National 4 & 5

Modern Studies

World Powers and International Issues

Frank Cooney
Paul Creaney
Gary Hughes
Pauline Kelly

HODDER
GIBSON
AN HACHETTE UK COMPANY

The Publishers would like to thank the following for permission to reproduce copyright material:

Photo credits p. 1 © EPAEuropean Press Photo Agency b.v./Alamy; p. 4 © Fotolia; pp. 4, 7, 8, 10, 11, 13 © TopFoto; p. 14 *l* © Fotolia *r* © Jim West/Alamy; p. 16 *l* © Zuma Press, Inc./Alamy *r* © Fotolia; p. 17 *l* © Fotolia *r* (P Diddy) © Charles Sykes/Rex Features, (Jesica Alba) © Dan Gorder/FilmMagic/Getty Images; p. 22 *t* © Visions of America/LLC/Alamy, *b* © Edward Parker/Alamy; p. 24 © Peter Titmuss/Alamy; p. 26 © Enigma/Alamy; pp. 27, 29 © Fotolia; p. 31 © Tetra Images/Alamy; p. 34 *t* © TopFoto *b* © Gallo Images/Alamy; p. 35 © Ulrich Doering/Alamy; p. 40 © Africa Media Online/Alamy; p. 42 *t* © Robin Laurance/Alamy, *b* © Gallo Images/Alamy; p. 44 © Reuters/Corbis; p. 45 © Hongqi Zhang/Alamy; p. 47 © TopFoto; p. 48 © Gallo Images/Alamy; p. 51 © Gallo Images/Alamy; p. 53 © Gallo Images/Alamy; p. 59 © Fotolia; pp. 62, 63 © TopFoto; p. 67 © Mark Henley/Panos Pictures; p. 71 © TopFoto; p. 73 © Quirky China News/Rex Features; p.76 © Imaginechina/Corbis; p. 80 © Fotolia; p. 85 © Karen Kasmauski/Corbis; p. 86 © Jennifer Reynolds; p. 89 © Joerg Boethling/Alamy; p. 90 © TopFoto; p. 91 © Zuma Press, Inc./Alamy; p. 98 © Jennifer Reynolds; p. 99 © War Child; pp. 100 © Oxfam; pp. 107, 109, 111 © TopFoto; p. 112 *tl* © dpa picture alliance archive/Alamy, *tr* © TopFoto; pp. 113, 114 © TopFoto; p. 116 © Propaganda/Alamy; p. 117 © TopFoto; p. 118 *t* © Fotolia, *b* © TopFoto; p. 120 © TopFoto; pp. 123, 125, 126,138 © David Sheerin.

Acknowledgements Page 99 War Child; page 100 Oxfam.

Every effort has been made to trace all copyright holders, but if any have been inadvertently overlooked the Publishers will be pleased to make the necessary arrangements at the first opportunity.

Although every effort has been made to ensure that website addresses are correct at time of going to press, Hodder Gibson cannot be held responsible for the content of any website mentioned in this book. It is sometimes possible to find a relocated web page by typing in the address of the home page for a website in the URL window of your browser.

Hachette UK's policy is to use papers that are natural, renewable and recyclable products and made from wood grown in sustainable forests. The logging and manufacturing processes are expected to confirm to the environmental regulations of the country of origin.

Orders: please contact Bookpoint Ltd, 130 Park Drive, Abingdon, Oxon OX14 4SE. Telephone: (44) 01235 827720. Fax: (44) 01235 400454. Lines are open 9.00–5.00, Monday to Saturday, with a 24-hour message answering service. Visit our website at www.hoddereducation.co.uk. Hodder Gibson can be contacted direct on: Tel: 0141 848 1609; Fax: 0141 889 6315; email: hoddergibson@hodder.co.uk

© Frank Cooney, Paul Creaney, Gary Hughes and Pauline Kelly 2014

First published in 2014 by

Hodder Gibson, an imprint of Hodder Education,
An Hachette UK Company
2a Christie Street
Paisley PA1 1NB

Impression number 5 4 3 2 1

Year   2018 2017 2016 2015 2014

Cover photo © Thinkstock – Getty Images/iStockphoto
Illustrations by Emma Golley at Redmoor Design and Integra Software Services Pvt. Ltd
Typeset by Integra, India
Printed in Italy

A catalogue record for this title is available from the British Library

ISBN: 978-1-4441-8261-3

Contents

What is the G20?

Which countries are members of the G20?

The **Group of Twenty**, or **G20**, represents more than 85% of the world's economy and includes countries from all over the globe. Membership consists of Argentina, Australia, Brazil, Canada, China, the European Union, France, Germany, India, Indonesia, Italy, Japan, Mexico, Russia, Saudi Arabia, South Africa, the Republic of Korea (South Korea), Turkey, the UK and the USA.

In this book, you will study one of following G20 members:

- the United States of America
- the Republic of South Africa
- the People's Republic of China.

The USA is the world's superpower, but China is fast emerging to challenge the USA's world economic dominance and its military dominance in Asia. South Africa is the regional economic and military superpower in southern Africa.

Figure 1.1 The G20 meeting in St Petersburg

> **What you will learn:**
> 1 Who belongs to the G20.
> 2 The importance and role of the G20.

FACT FILE

What is the G20?

- The G20 is made up of 19 of the world's largest economies, together with a representative from the European Union.
- Meetings are held once a year in the country of the current president of the group.
- The first meeting, or summit, took place in the US capital Washington DC in November 2008. The idea was originally proposed by former Canadian Prime Minister Paul Martin.
- Finance ministers usually meet around the world, although G20 leaders sometimes take part instead.
- Russia held the latest G20 meeting in St Petersburg in September 2013.

What is the role of the G20?

The G20 members talk about the most important **financial** and **economic** issues of the day. Since 2010 those have mainly been the **global recession**, which is being felt by most regions of the world. Other topics include improving **food security** in poor regions and **sustainable development**.

The organisation has three main objectives:

- To co-ordinate policy between its members in order to achieve global economic stability and promote sustainable growth.
- To promote financial regulations that reduce risks and prevent future financial crises.
- To create new ways of carrying out international agreements and financial transactions.

The G20 Summit of 2012

The 2012 G20 Summit was held in Los Cabos in Mexico. After two days of discussions and meetings with leaders from the world's major economies, US President Barack Obama held a press conference. He said the Summit 'has been an opportunity for us to hear from European leaders on the progress they're making and on their next steps … It's also been a chance for the international community, including the United States – the largest economy in the world, and with our own record of responding to financial crises – to stress the importance of decisive action at this moment.'

ICT task

Watch a video clip of President Obama discussing his main thoughts and outlining the USA's future actions at www.whitehouse.gov/blog/2012/06/20/president-obama-speaks-end-g20-summit

www

For further information on the G20, go to www.g20.org

Show your understanding

1 (a) Why is the G20 so powerful?
   (b) What issues do its members discuss?

Branch out

2 Hold a G20 summit in your classroom.

(a) In pairs or groups of three, choose a G20 country. Make sure that other class members have chosen different countries.

(b) Research your G20 country on the Internet. Try to find information on the following points.

- Is your G20 country rich or poor? What evidence can you find to back up your view?
- In terms of your G20 country, think of the health system, the economy (GDP), education, etc. Carry out some research on these aspects.
- Does your G20 country follow a dictatorship regime or a democratically elected government? Provide evidence to support your claim.
- Is there any evidence to suggest that your G20 country helps poor countries or supports charity organisations?

(c) In your groups, create four recommendations or questions that your G20 country would like to discuss at the next summit. Use the following points as a guide to help you.

- How can the G20 improve health or education issues in developing countries? Explain solutions and ideas that your G20 country would like to share or discuss.
- How can the G20 find a way to resolve the current economic crisis?
- How can the G20 help to reduce poverty throughout the world?
- How can the G20 improve trade between countries?

Chapter 2

The United States of America

The USA as a superpower and its relevance to Scotland

The USA as a global superpower

The definition of a **superpower** in international politics is not very different from the definition of a superhero in the comic book world. A superhero has no equal or rival among the general public; the only person who competes with the power of a superhero is another superhero or a super villain.

Until the collapse of the Soviet Union in the 1990s, the USA and the Soviet Union shared the title of superpowers and competed for influence around the world. This was known as the **Cold War**. The USA and the Soviet Union both had nuclear weapon capabilities and this made everyone fearful.

It was a competition between the **capitalist** USA and the **communist** Soviet Union to see who would dominate the world. They each believed that their own system of government and economics was the best way to run a country. One of the major differences between capitalism and communism is with regard to the **resources** or the **means of production**.

The impact of capitalism in the USA:

★ People can own their own businesses.
★ People can express their own views, opinions and religious beliefs.
★ People can elect their own government.
★ People can choose to pay for private education and health care.

What you will learn:

1 Why the USA is a global superpower.
2 Why the USA is relevant to Scotland.

A **superpower** is a powerful and influential nation, especially a nuclear power that dominates its allies or client states in an international power bloc. It has the ability to militarily, politically and economically influence all areas of the world:

- militarily – army
- politically – government
- economically – wealth.

The **Cold War** is the term used to describe the relationship between the two superpowers after the Second World War came to an end in 1945. The word 'cold' emphasises the fact that war never actually broke out between the two countries but that both countries were hostile to one another.

In **capitalism**, much of the country's resources or the means of production lies with a private owner. The profit in a capitalist structure belongs to the private owner only.

In **communism**, the community or society solely owns all of the country's resources or the means of production such as businesses, factories and minerals. The profit of any enterprise is shared equally by all the people.

USA: WORLD SUPERPOWER

Figure 2.1 The USA flag

The USA is still the most powerful nation on Earth. It has the highest GDP of any world economy at over $15 trillion (China lags behind in second place on $11 trillion). The demographic profile is healthy, with over a quarter of Americans below the age of 20. Its military prowess straddles the planet — the USA spends $711 billion on its military every year and has a huge stockpile of nuclear weapons.

Show your understanding

Refer to *USA: World superpower* (above). What evidence supports this viewpoint? Compare your answer with a partner.

National Tartan Day

In 1998 the US Congress designated 6 April as National Tartan Day to celebrate the contributions to America by Scottish-Americans. The date is the anniversary of the **Declaration of Arbroath** in 1320, one of the first documents in the world to declare a right to freedom. The Annual Tartan Week celebrations come to life every April with the largest celebration taking place in New York City. Thousands descend onto the streets of the Big Apple to celebrate their heritage, culture and the impact of the Scottish Americans in the USA today.

Figure 2.2 A Tartan Day parade in New York City

The USA's relevance to Scotland

The 2010 US Community Census stated that 29 million American citizens claimed Scottish heritage, with the majority of these residing in southern states such as Tennessee, North and South Carolina and Texas. Americans of Scottish descent have played a vibrant and influential role in the development of the USA. From the framers of the **Declaration of Independence** to the first man on the Moon, Scottish-Americans have contributed mightily to the fields of the arts, science, politics, law, and more. These are the people and the accomplishments that are honoured on National Tartan Day.

Show your understanding

1 Explain why the USA and the Soviet Union were called superpowers.
2 In your own words, describe why the Cold War was different from other wars.
3 In your own words, explain the difference between capitalism and communism.
4 Why is the USA relevant to Scotland?

Branch out

5 Think of all of the influences that the USA has had on the Scottish people and its culture. Write down a list of examples and compare them with a partner.

The USA today

> **What you will learn:**
>
> 1 The background to the USA.
> 2 Who makes up the American population.
> 3 The push and pull factors that encourage people to come to the USA, and immigration issues.
> 4 What the American Dream is.

The background to the USA

The USA is the fourth largest country in the word. It covers an area of 9,826,657 km². Russia, Canada and China are the only countries that have a larger land mass than the USA. There are 50 states that make up the USA, with Alaska and Hawaii being

ICT task

1 Go to the website www.50states.com

2 From the Home page, scroll down so that you can see the State List (light blue background). Do not click on any of the states.

3 Find the name of the capital city for the following six states (just hover your cursor over the state's name): Colorado, Iowa, New Mexico, North Carolina, Virginia and Wisconsin.

4 Go to the *State Facts* link at the menu bar at the top of the page and select *State Flags*. Spend a few minutes looking at the flags and choose your favourite. Explain why this is your favourite flag.

5 Choose **one** state and find out the following pieces of information:

- admission to statehood (when it became a state)
- which states border it
- economy – agriculture and industry.

Figure 2.3 The states of the USA

separated from the mainland. The USA experiences a variety of landscapes and climates and there are six different time zones, including Alaska and Hawaii.

Who makes up the American population?

The USA is a diverse country. There are millions of people who would call themselves American, even though they may not have been born on US soil. American society has often been described as a 'melting point' or 'salad bowl' as there are many different ethnic groups that make up the population of the USA.

To understand the term **'melting pot'**, think about making a cup of coffee. You may use hot water, coffee granules, milk and sugar. You stir them all together and get a brown liquid. You will not be able to pick out any of the ingredients. People who go to live in the USA may be Scottish, Japanese or Mexican, but they can lose their own identity after a period of time and become 'American'.

For the **'salad bowl'**, when you make a salad you may add lettuce, red onions, green peppers, cucumber and tomatoes. You can mix them all together in a bowl, but you are still able to pick out the individual ingredients. Is it possible for people from different ethnic groups and cultures to 'become American' but also keep their own identities?

The ethnic composition of the USA

Between 1980 and 2008, the racial/ethnic composition of the USA shifted: the white population declined from 80% of the total population to 66%; the Hispanic/Latino population increased from 6% of the total population to 15%; the African-American/black population remained at about 12%; and the Asian/Pacific Islander population increased from less than 2% of the total population to 4%. In 2008, Native Americans made up about 1% and people of two or more races made up a further 1% of the population.

The US population is made up of five main ethnic groups (see Figure 2.4). In January 2013, the total population was estimated at 315,192,552. The population is rising by approximately 1% each year.

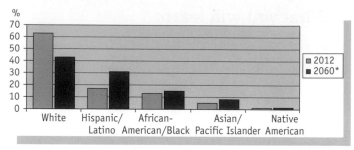

Figure 2.4 Percentage of population in the USA by five main ethnic groups, December 2012

* Predicted

Source: United States Census Bureau

 Show your understanding

1 What is the estimated population of the USA? Why do you think the figure is just an estimate?

2 Read the 'melting pot' theory and the 'salad bowl' theory. Which theory do you feel best explains people who 'become American' when they move to the USA? Explain your answer.

3 Which ethnic group is the fastest-growing group in the USA? Provide evidence from Figure 2.4.

4 Write down the five main ethnic groups in the USA. For each group, write down:
   (a) which country/countries the ethnic group originated from
   (b) the most recent population figures.

Branch out

5 Can you think of famous Americans from different ethnic groups? Working in pairs, write down the five main groups and list as many famous Americans as you can think of. Compare your list with other pairs in your class.

Develop your skills

6 'Hispanics/Latinos are the fastest-growing group in the USA. There is no evidence to suggest that the ethnic minority groups will ever catch up to the white population.' (E. Woods)
   Using Figure 2.4, give one reason to support and one reason to oppose this view.

FACT FILE

The main ethnic groups

Figure 2.5 The population of the USA has a diverse ethnic mix

- **Whites**: the largest ethnic group in the USA. Until 1860, most migrants to the USA were from northern Europe. These people settled into different parts of America. Between 1860 and 1920, white migrants came mainly from eastern and southern Europe. Many of these people lived and worked in built-up city areas. Migrants from the UK, Ireland and Germany were three of the favoured countries to achieve entry into the USA.

- **Hispanics/Latinos**: originate from Spanish-speaking countries such as Mexico, Cuba and Puerto Rico.
  - **Mexicans**: make up the largest group. They are concentrated in the western and southern border states such as Texas, Arizona and California. Many illegal immigrants enter the USA from Mexico.
  - **Cubans**: 80% of Cubans in the USA live in the south – mainly in Florida and particularly in Miami. Florida is 145 km (90 miles) from Cuba. Cubans fled to the USA to seek political refuge when Fidel Castro took over. Many Cubans call themselves exiles, not immigrants, because they intend to return to Cuba.

- **Puerto Ricans**: many live in the mid-Atlantic, mainly in New York. Puerto Rico is a Free Associated State of the USA, which entitles Puerto Ricans to enter mainland USA to work and live.

- **African-Americans/blacks**: in the USA the majority of blacks live in the south. Most live in the south for historical reasons as it was the centre of slavery in the nineteenth century. From the 1940s to the 1970s, blacks migrated from the south to the cities of the north and west, but since the 1970s this movement has reversed and increasing numbers are moving to the south from cities in the north. They are moving back to escape the poverty and segregation that still exists in northern cities. The south offers an improved lifestyle.

- **Asians/Pacific Islanders**: immigrants, or descendants of immigrants, arrived on the west coast of America from Far East countries such as China, Japan and Korea over the past 150 years. The majority have settled in the cities of the west and south.

- **Native Americans**: this group are the 'original' Americans. In the 2000 census, Native American was the group name given to American Indian, Eskimo and Aleut. (The Eskimo and the Aleut inhabit Alaska.) Reservations are recognised in US law as foreign territories and they are not subject to all the laws of the USA.

Push and pull factors

Push and pull factors are often used to explain why people move to the USA. **Push factors** are reasons why they are being 'pushed' out of their own country. **Pull factors** are reasons why they are 'pulled' or attracted to the USA.

Push factors

Dictatorship

Unemployment

No land

Poor health care

Poverty

Lack of housing

Little or no educational opportunities

War and natural disasters

Figure 2.6 Push and pull factors

Pull factors

Democratic country

Freedom of speech

Wealth

Land

The American Dream

Education

Health care

Jobs

Capitalism

✍ Show your understanding

Branch out

1 Working in pairs, write down three push factors that you feel are the most important reasons for a person to leave their country. Write down an explanation for each of your chosen push factors.
2 Write down three pull factors that you think that most people would be attracted to. Write down an explanation for each of your chosen pull factors.

Immigration

Figure 2.7 Mexican border patrol

Arguments for immigration

- Some of the most intelligent and ambitious individuals, who are unsatisfied with their own countries, bring their skills to the USA.
- It increases the diversity and expands the culture of the country.
- Immigrants often take low-paying jobs, such as food service and hotel cleaning, which many Americans do not want to do at such low wages.
- It improves the overall image of the USA internationally, as it is seen as an open, welcoming country, and immigrants who return home or maintain contact with family back home have a true image of the USA.
- It gives struggling people all over the world an opportunity for a better life. This country was built on immigrants who sought opportunity, political and religious freedom.

Arguments against immigration

- More immigrants may result in more opportunities for terrorists, drug dealers and other criminals to enter the country.

- Immigrants – especially poorer ones – use high levels of government resources, such as health care, education and welfare without paying taxes or a high rate of taxes.
- The national identity and language is disappearing.
- Emigration to the USA hurts the country that is left as many of the male population, workers, and top intellectuals often leave.
- Less-skilled American citizens earn less money and have fewer job opportunities because they must compete with immigrants in the job market.

Extract from President Obama's State of the Union Address, 2011

'Today, there are hundreds of thousands of students excelling in our schools who are not American citizens. Some are the children of undocumented workers, who had nothing to do with the actions of their parents. They grew up as Americans and pledge allegiance to our flag, and yet they live every day with the threat of deportation.

I am prepared to work with Republicans and Democrats to protect our borders, enforce our laws and address the millions of undocumented workers who are now living in the shadows. Let's stop expelling talented, responsible young people who could be staffing our research labs or starting a new business, who could be further enriching this nation.

We may have different backgrounds, but we believe in the same dream that says this is a country where anything is possible, no matter who you are, no matter where you come from.'

Illegal immigration: Mexican border fence

After the 9/11 attacks (see page 109), further efforts were taken by Homeland Security to strengthen border security. In 2006 the Secure Fence Act was passed to build 1100 km (700 miles) of double-reinforced security fencing in areas along the border with Mexico prone to drug trafficking and illegal immigration. President Bush also deployed 6,000 National Guardsmen to the Mexican border to assist with border control.

The scheme was intended to be fully operational by 2011. However, it has become a major headache for both the Bush and the Obama administrations. Technical problems plagued the project and plans to complete it halted at the end of 2011.

According to the Department of Homeland Security, taxpayers have spent $1bn (£632m) on the technology which only protects 85 km (53 miles) of border.

 Added value

'Immigration is beneficial for social and economic development in the USA.' Research and investigate the arguments for and against this statement. You could present your findings in a word-processed booklet illustrated with tables, graphs and images.

You might wish to consider the following aims:

- to find out the social and economic arguments to support this hypothesis
- to find out the social and economic arguments to oppose this hypothesis
- to consider to what extent the evidence examined is exaggerated or biased
- to come to your own conclusion based on the reliability of evidence.

Show your understanding

Branch out

Write down the main arguments for and against immigration. Hold a class discussion or debate on your findings.

The American Dream

The **American Dream** is the idea that any American citizen, however poor their background, can aim to succeed by working hard. The American system of free enterprise capitalism encourages people to set up their own business with the incentive of becoming wealthy and successful. In the USA, success is admired. Many come to the country in hope of achieving the American Dream.

One example of a successful American is Mark Zuckerberg, a computer programmer and Internet entrepreneur. He is best known as one of five co-founders of the social networking website, Facebook.

Figure 2.8 Mark Zuckerberg

 Show your understanding

Branch out

1 Carry out some research and write down song lyrics or words that you associate with the idea of the American Dream.

2 Write down lyrics that could show that the American Dream does not exist.

3 Working in pairs, think of your own lyrics that could be used to write a song about 'Achieving the Scottish Dream'.

Group presentation

4 In groups, complete a poster presentation on someone who you believe has achieved the American Dream. Think of famous people who have achieved this ideal – perhaps someone who is not an American but who has made their fortune in the USA, or someone who was from a poor background but who is now rich and famous, or the first ever black president …

   (a) Organise yourselves into groups of three.

   (b) Choose someone who you all think has achieved the American Dream.

   (c) Assign yourselves with these roles: researcher, poster designer and presenter. Help each other with these roles, but each person is responsible for making sure that their role is completed.

You will be assessed on your poster and presentation. As a class, think of your success criteria – what would you expect from a great poster presentation? Consider the following:

- the poster layout: great use of pictures, bold and bright headings, plenty of information, but not too small – can the people at the back of the class read it?
- what form the presentation will take: who will speak and when? What else could accompany the presentation – songs, video clips?
- speech: loud and clear voices, keep eye contact with the audience, do not read from the poster, create cards that you can read your information from.

The Constitution and government

> **What you will learn:**
>
> 1 The meaning of the term 'the Constitution'.
> 2 The main system of government.

What is the Constitution?

In the eighteenth century, the Americans managed to defeat the British to gain their independence in the War of Independence. In 1783 America was left with no government, so the original 13 colonies (the 13 original states) agreed to devise a new form of government – a federal state. This federal state would unite all the states, resulting in the name 'the United States of America'.

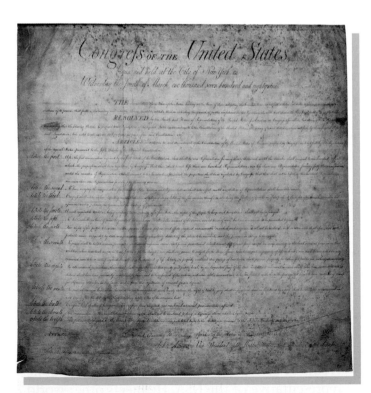

Figure 2.9 The original Bill of Rights consists of ten amendments to the Constitution

The Constitution is a set of rules that outlines how the government should be run. It is a written document that is the basis for the American system of government. It is also the basis of the legal system in the USA, with all laws stemming from the Constitution in some way.

Since the original document was written, there have been several amendments, or changes to the Constitution. The first amendments, added in 1791, were intended to protect individual freedoms and rights and are known collectively as the **Bill of Rights**.

FACT FILE

Examples from the Bill of Rights

1st Amendment: freedom of religion, speech and the press, and the right to peaceful assembly

2nd Amendment: the right to keep and bear arms

5th Amendment: the rights of persons accused of a serious offence to be heard before a grand jury and the right to remain silent

6th Amendment: the right to a speedy and public trial by an impartial jury

8th Amendment: freedom from cruel and unusual punishment

The US system of government

The Constitution outlined that power would be divided between the national (federal) government and the individual states. The Constitution also defines the powers and duties of the three main branches of government:

- the **legislative** branch – Congress
- the **executive** branch – the president
- the **judicial** branch – the Supreme Court.

The Constitution is the supreme laws in the land. It defines the relationship and allocation of powers between the three main branches. The **separation of powers** ensures that no one branch can become

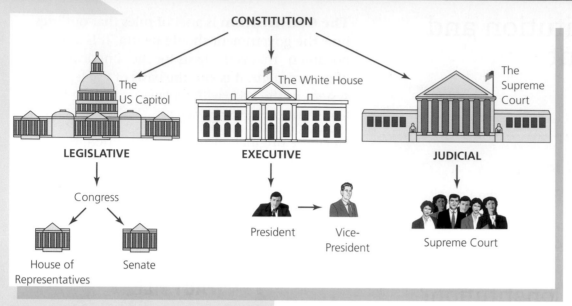

Figure 2.10 The system of government in the USA

too powerful because all the power is distributed equally to all three branches. Each branch must agree with one another on an issue before a decision can be formally approved. It is a system of **checks and balances**. No single branch can impose its will. This can make it difficult to achieve an outcome or to reach decisions, and is quite different to what was originally intended when the Constitution was set up (see *Budget Crisis 2013–2014*).

Budget crisis 2013–14

In October 2013 the conflict between Republicans and President Obama and his Democratic party led to the partial shutdown of the US government for 16 days. Around 800,000 non-essential staff at federal agencies were sent home (out of 2.8 million federal staff). The government faced the prospect of running out of money. Republicans in the House of Representatives had created the crisis by trying to link their acceptance of the budget to Obama delaying his healthcare reforms (see page 23) for 1 year. Obama refused, saying that Congress had passed his health reforms and he would not be blackmailed. A temporary settlement was reached to ensure the government would remain open.

The president

The president of the USA has a role in all three branches of government. He can suggest policy to Congress and he can also approve any policy that Congress presents to him; he is head of the executive; and he can appoint judges to the Supreme Court.

- **Chief legislator**: he is expected to propose legislation to Congress for new laws. The president can refuse to sign (**veto**) a bill if he does not feel is in the interest of the people. However, Congress can override the veto with a two-thirds majority in both the House of Representatives and the Senate.

- **Commander-in-chief of the armed forces**: the president is the head of national security. He is the commanding general of the world's most powerful military forces and can order the use of troops overseas. Congress has the power to declare war with another country.

- **Chief executive**: he is responsible for the running the federal government. He appoints thousands of people to the federal government. The president has a duty to uphold the decisions made by the Supreme Court – he is the 'guardian of the Constitution'.

- **Head of state**: the president is the chief public representative of the USA. He meets other world leaders and negotiates treaties with them.

I do solemnly swear that I will faithfully execute the Office of President of the United States, and will, to the best of my ability, preserve, protect and defend the Constitution of the United States.

Figure 2.11 All presidents must take the oath of office

Presidents are elected for periods or 'terms' of four years. A president can only be elected to office twice, which means someone can only be in office for a maximum of eight years.

The presidential **veto** is a power vested in the president by which he can return a bill to Congress unsigned.

Congressional elections occur every two years. Every member of the House of Representatives and one-third of the Senate stands for re-election in any given election year. A presidential election is held every fourth year – 2012, 2016, 2020 etc.

ICT task

1 Go to the website www.whitehouse.gov

2 Go to the *White House* link on the menu bar at the top of the page and select *Presidents*.

3 Choose one of the 44 presidents and write down the following information:

   (a) The name of your chosen president and their chronological position.

   (b) When did they serve as president?

   (c) When were they born and where did they grow up?

   (d) What did they do before becoming president?

   (e) Describe a few decisions they made as president.

Show your understanding

1 What is the Constitution?

2 Describe what the Bill of Rights is.

3 Make a simple copy of the government diagram (Figure 2.10).

4 When are congressional and presidential elections held?

Branch out

5 In pairs, discuss why the Constitution outlined that there must be three separate branches of government.

Develop your skills

6 'The president of the United States is the most powerful person in government. He is solely responsible for law-making decisions.' (*M. Duncan*)

To what extent might M. Duncan be accused of exaggeration?

Laws, rights and responsibilities

What you will learn:

1 Different examples of federal and state laws.

2 The rights and responsibilities of the American people.

Most Americans have more daily contact with their state and local governments than with federal (national) government. Police departments, libraries, and schools — not to mention driving licenses and parking tickets — usually fall under the oversight of state and county (local) governments. Each state has its own written constitution and these documents are often far more elaborate than their federal counterpart.

Federal government

The federal government makes laws for all the people in the 50 states. It is responsible for a number of key areas that affect every citizen:

- the US currency – every state uses dollars and cents
- the armed forces – the military and navy are used by all citizens in each state
- the postal service – every state uses the same postal service, just as the UK has the Royal Mail postal service
- treaties and foreign relations with other countries.

Figure 2.12 The federal government is responsible for several key areas

State government

Each of the 50 states has its own laws for certain state issues. It may be surprising that individual states have different age restrictions, for example, and use different methods of capital punishment.

- Executions – some states still have capital punishment and each uses a variety of execution methods.
- Marriage laws – states have different marriage age consents, ranging from 14 to 21.
- Gun ownership – states have different restrictions regarding gun ownership.
- Education – some states vary in the age at which students start and leave school.

Figure 2.13 States have different restrictions regarding gun ownership

Rights and responsibilities

As the USA is a democratic country, all citizens are given rights and privileges, but with rights come responsibilities. The following are examples of the rights, privileges and responsibilities of all US citizens. In some states, some rights and privileges may have some restrictions for some categories of citizens.

Rights

A right is a freedom that is protected. Citizens of different countries have different rights. In the USA, the first ten amendments to the Constitution are known as the Bill of Rights (see page 11). These enshrine certain freedoms and rights that cannot be taken away from anyone.

However, some citizens feel that their rights are now being limited:

- Members of the National Rifle Association are unhappy with the restrictions placed on gun control.
- Many ethnic minorities feel that their voting rights will be reduced with changes made to the Voting Rights Act. Southern states can now bring in their own electoral laws, which might indirectly discriminate against minority groups, such as the requirement to provide photographic identification in order to vote.

Responsibilities

A responsibility is a duty or something someone should do. When people work to help the whole community, they work for the common good. Obeying federal, state and local laws is an important responsibility, but there are many others including:

- to respect the rights, beliefs and opinions of others
- to register and use your vote.

The right to own guns brings the responsibility to use them only in self-defence.

 Show your understanding

1 Explain why US citizens are given rights and privileges.
2 Which document ensures that the rights of American citizens cannot be taken away from them?
3 Write down three rights and their matching responsibilities.

Branch out

4 In pairs:
   (a) find out which states have age restrictions for marriage
   (b) write down a list of states that use capital punishment as a form of punishment.

Political participation

What you will learn:

1 That the USA is a democracy.
2 How American people can participate in politics.
3 The main political parties and where they get their support.

What is a democracy?

The USA prides itself on being a democracy. This means that people have the opportunity to participate in politics at all levels. From local upwards, the main types of government elected are county, state and federal.

In addition, Americans vote for individual positions ranging from local officials right up to the president. Presidential elections take place every four years, and it is not unusual for a president to be elected from one party whereas Congress (the **Senate** and the **House of Representatives**) is dominated by the other main party. The two main parties in the USA are the **Republicans** and the **Democrats**.

US citizens vote for someone to make decisions on their behalf – a representative democracy. There are currently over 315 million American citizens who rely on the president and other representatives to make decisions in their best interests.

How can US citizens participate in politics?

There are many ways in which American people can participate in politics, including:

- voting in federal, state and county elections
- standing as a candidate for a political party
- joining a political party and helping during election campaigns
- contacting their elected representatives, for example by telephone, letter or email
- contributing to party funds
- joining an interest group (or pressure group), for example the National Rifle Association (NRA)
- taking part in a protest or demonstration.

Americans can join **interest groups**. These groups put pressure on the government to amend or introduce laws in support of their cause. The members participate in marches and demonstrations, organise petitions, letter campaigns, media campaigns and other forms of lobbying in order to gain public awareness and support.

Figure 2.14 US citizens can participate in politics by joining an interest group such as the NRA

There are frequent elections in America and the fact that the presidential election campaign lasts for a year means that campaigning is crucial to the political process. A US citizen or organisation may choose to support a political party financially, which means giving the party money.

Who can US citizens vote for in elections?

American citizens can vote in elections to the federal government. This controls national and international affairs. Political candidates are elected to Congress, which is made up of the Senate (100 senators) and the House of Representatives (435 congressmen). Citizens can also vote for the president. They can also vote in state elections to elect state governors and representatives to the state assemblies. At local level, they can vote in county elections for sheriffs, tax collectors, judges, district attorneys and even dog catchers.

By registering as a Democrat or a Republican, voters can participate in primary elections, which are part of the process of choosing the party's candidate for president.

The main political parties

FACT FILE

The Democrat Party

Figure 2.15 The Democrats' logo

The Democrat Party 'is committed to keeping [our] nation safe and expanding opportunity for every American'. Support is concentrated in coastal areas and major cities. The party typically gets its support from blue-collar manual workers; urban dwellers; Catholics; Jews; racial minority and poorer groups; women; those with liberal viewpoints.

The Republican Party

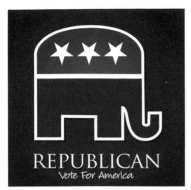

Figure 2.16 The Republicans' logo

The Republican Party believes that 'people can succeed through hard work, family support and self-discipline'. It is the party of big business. The party typically gains support from white-collar, professional workers; the Midwest and the South in more rural and suburban areas; more middle and higher income earners; Protestants (especially evangelicals); whites; males; college-educated; those with conservative views including the religious right.

The Center for the Study of the American Electorate put 2012 **voting turnout** at 57.5% of all **eligible voters**. This turnout was lower than the 2008 presidential election when 62.3% of Americans cast their votes. In 2004, 60.4% of citizens cast their ballots. The evidence shows that not all eligible voters actually use their votes even in extremely important elections such as helping to elect the president of the USA.

In the 2012 presidential election, it was estimated that 126 million people voted in the election, when President Barack Obama defeated Mitt Romney. Therefore, approximately 93 million eligible citizens did not use their vote to decide who would be their president for the next four years.

The youth vote

In the UK, people are included on the electoral register as soon as they are 18 years old and therefore eligible to vote. However, Americans have to make the effort to register themselves; they are not automatically given the vote. This could explain why voter registration is low for some groups.

There have been numerous campaigns over the years that have tried to encourage people to register. The 'Vote or Die' and 'Declare Yourself' campaigns have tried to influence younger potential voters to register.

Figure 2.17 Examples of two campaigns that have tried to encourage young people to vote: P Diddy supporting the 'Vote or Die' campaign and Jessica Alba taking part in the 'Declare Yourself' campaign

Voting turnout is the percentage of eligible voters who cast a ballot in an election.

Eligible voters are defined differently in different countries and the term should not be confused with the total adult population.

Why are ethnic minorities less likely to participate?

Not all groups in the USA participate equally in politics. All ethnic minorities are less likely to be involved in politics – whether as voters, campaigners or as candidates – than white Americans. Ethnic minorities are also under-represented in political positions. In the past, many ethnic minority groups were discouraged from voting as many politicians aimed their policies at the white majority. Nowadays, more Hispanics and African-Americans turn out to vote. However, many African-Americans still feel politics is irrelevant to their lives. Political participation tends to be higher in areas where African-American candidates have a chance of winning. Certain elections seem to motivate the voters and get them to turn out at the polls. For example, in the 2008 general election there was an increase in the number of young people and ethnic minorities.

WWW

For information on Rock the Vote, go to www.rockthevote.org

In 2008 Barack Obama was elected president of the USA. Until then, African-Americans had made little impact at national political level. There had never been an African-American president or vice-president, and the official Democratic and Republican candidates for these offices had always been white.

The 2012 Presidential election

President Obama's second term in the White House was largely secured by record numbers of votes from ethnic minorities, whereas his popularity among whites appeared to have decreased.

- Obama received 65.9 million votes compared to Romney's 60.9 million. The electoral college result exaggerated Obama's popular vote, with Romney only receiving 206 votes to Obama's 332.

Show your understanding

1 (a) What is an interest group?
   (b) Describe what members of an interest group may get involved in.
2 Give an example of who citizens can vote for in federal, state and county elections.
3 Describe a typical Democrat supporter.
4 Describe a typical Republican supporter.
5 Why are ethnic minorities less likely to be involved in politics and to what extent is this changing?

Branch out

6 Will you vote when you finally get the opportunity? Explain your answer.
7 (a) What do you think would encourage young people to vote?
   (b) In pairs, create a leaflet that outlines your campaign. Try to include the following;
   - a catchy slogan or motto
   - the reasons why young people should use their vote and ways to encourage young people to vote through advertising – how you would advertise your campaign.

Develop your skills

8 In pairs, draw a mind map that outlines the ways in which US citizens participate in politics.

- Hispanics accounted for 10% of all voters in the election. Of these, 71% voted for Obama, up from 67% in 2008. In a sign Republicans are failing to win over this increasingly influential group, Romney won just 27%.

- A record number of Asian voters – 3% of the electorate – also turned out, with nearly three-quarters backing Obama. He also won a staggering 93% of African-American votes.

- Obama received just 39% of the white votes, down by 4% on the last election, a drop his campaign had anticipated.

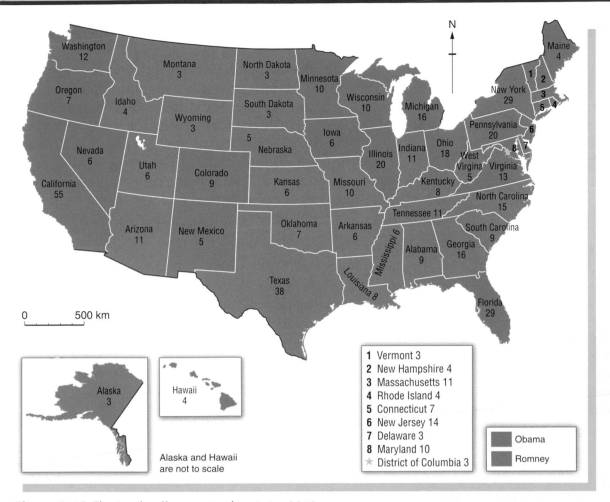

Figure 2.18 Electoral college votes by state, 2012

Map legend:
1 Vermont 3
2 New Hampshire 4
3 Massachusetts 11
4 Rhode Island 4
5 Connecticut 7
6 New Jersey 14
7 Delaware 3
8 Maryland 10
★ District of Columbia 3

Obama
Romney

Alaska and Hawaii are not to scale

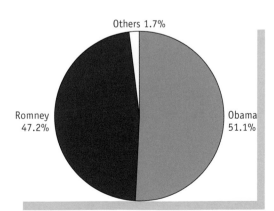

Figure 2.19 Voting by American people (%), 2012

Others 1.7%
Romney 47.2%
Obama 51.1%

Show your understanding

1 Why was the ethnic minority vote so crucial in the 2012 presidential election?

Develop your skills

2 'Obama's victory in both the popular vote and the electoral college vote was overwhelming.' (*An American reporter*)

To what extent does the evidence in Figures 2.18 and 2.19 support this view?

Social and economic issues

What you will learn:

1 The social and economic issues that exist in the USA.
2 Government reaction and responses to social and economic issues.

The USA prides itself on a free enterprise economy and the idea that all citizens are born equal and thus anyone can achieve the American Dream (see page 10). Although hard work and self-help can enable American citizens to prosper and succeed, this is not the reality for many ethnic minorities. The USA is an **unequal society** and millions of Americans live in poverty.

Education

Educational attainment is an important factor in determining employment and income levels. As whites have higher educational attainment, more whites will end up with better paid jobs.

Why are there inequalities and who experiences them?

Generally, half of the money that is required to operate schools comes from the state, and the remaining half is raised through local property and sales taxes. Those communities that have high property values can provide high quality facilities, the latest software and the best teachers, whereas poorer districts find it difficult to fund even the basics. Schools in ghettos and *barrios* (poor neighbourhoods) are substandard and are short of resources as well as teachers.

A lack of role models and home encouragement makes learning all the more difficult, creating a **cycle of poverty**. A lack of money also leads to problems as students have no access to technology.

The following factors have a huge impact on education attainment for certain groups.

- **Location**: in the past few decades, white students were concentrated in suburban and rural areas, with lower percentages in cities and towns. Black, Hispanic and Asian/Pacific Islander students were concentrated in cities and suburban areas.

- **Poverty**: in 2010–11, 48% of fourth graders were eligible for free or subsidised lunches, including 77% of Hispanic, 74% of black, 68% of American

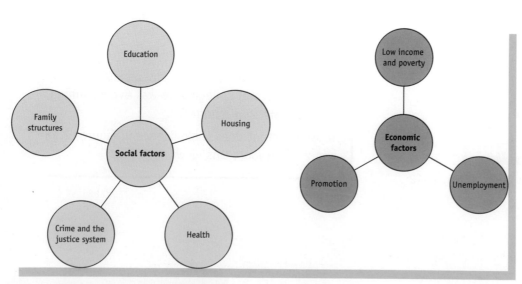

Figure 2.20 Factors of social and economic inequality

Indian/Alaska Native, 34% of Asian/Pacific Islander and 29% of white students.

- **Language barriers**: in 2010, about 69% of Hispanic and 64% of Asian elementary/secondary school students spoke a language other than English at home. About 18% of Hispanic and 17% of Asian students spoke English with difficulty, compared with 7% of Native Hawaiians or other Pacific Islanders, 3% of American Indians/Alaska Natives and 1% each of whites and blacks.

- **Status dropout rates by race/ethnicity**: the 2009 status dropout rate for Asians/Pacific Islanders (3.4%) was the lowest among the racial/ethnic groups. Whites had the next lowest rate (5.2%). The black status dropout rate (9.3%) was lower than the rate for Hispanics (17.6%).

Government responses

Educational inequality has become one of the most important political and social issues in the USA. There have been numerous attempts at reforms and there continue to be more. With different causes that are deeply rooted in history, society and culture, this inequality is difficult to eradicate.

The American Recovery Reinvestment Act (2012)

The US Government stated that this Act has invested heavily in education as a way both to provide jobs and lay the foundation for long-term prosperity.

- The Act provides $77 billion for reforms to strengthen elementary and secondary education.

- It aims to make improvements in teacher effectiveness and ensure that all schools have highly qualified teachers.

- It will improve achievement in low-performing schools, through support and effective interventions.

- The Act includes $30 billion to address college affordability and improve access to higher education.

In 2008 about 29% of American adults (25 years of age or older) had at least a bachelor's degree, including 52% of Asian/Pacific Islanders, 33% of whites, 20% of blacks, 13% of Hispanics and 15% of American Indian/Alaska Natives.

Show your understanding

1. Summarise the main reasons why there are inequalities in education in the USA.
2. Why is location an important factor when looking at inequalities in education?
3. Explain the reasons why some ethnic minorities may experience substandard education.
4. What is the government doing to try to reduce inequalities in education?

Housing

There are huge differences in terms of houses and neighbourhoods in the USA. Housing can have a huge impact on citizens' lives.

Why are there inequalities?

Ghettos

A **ghetto**, also known as 'the hood' or the inner city, is a part of an American city where nearly everyone is from an ethnic minority. Most ghettos are poor, but not all. Some of the black parts of Queens in New York, for example, are richer than some of the white parts. Ghettos often suffer from the following problems:

- increasing rates of unemployment
- poverty
- violence and gang culture
- drug trafficking
- deteriorating houses
- environmental issues, such as rubbish being left on the street.

Figure 2.21 Contrasting visions of the USA

Suburbs

Suburbs are on the outer edges of a city. People living in the same suburb usually share similar backgrounds with regard to race, socio-economic status and age. The houses that make up the area are often similar in appearance, size and blueprint, a layout design referred to as 'tract housing' or 'cookie-cutter housing'.

As the suburbs grew, more and more of the middle classes abandoned the inner cities. The suburbs were attractive for many reasons:

- fresh new buildings
- clean streets
- better-funded schools
- sense of security
- less crime
- less poverty.

Government responses

Department of Housing and Urban Development (HUD)

In order to achieve strong, sustainable, inclusive communities and quality, affordable homes for all, the **Department of Housing and Urban Development (HUD)** has developed a portfolio of programmes and policy initiatives to meet housing and development challenges.

- 72% rental assistance provides an ongoing stream of funding that makes up the gap between what low income tenants can afford to pay in rent and the cost of housing.
- The overall HUD budget of $47.9 billion is said to provide direct housing and services to millions of families and thousands of communities across the country.

 Show your understanding

1 Describe what life can be like in the ghettos.
2 Describe what life can be like in the suburbs.
3 Which one would you prefer to live in? Explain your answer.

Health

Americans are not all equal when it comes to their health. **Private health care** ensures that those with money have the opportunity to be healthier than poor Americans.

Why are there inequalities?

Unlike in the UK, the USA does not have a National Health Service (NHS) that is free to use. American citizens pay for their medical bills through private medical insurance: they have to pay for their health care.

- There were 49.9 million uninsured Americans in 2010, making up 16.3% of the total population.
- The number of those who did have private medical insurance was 256.2 million in 2010.
- It is estimated that 26.9% of people earning less than $25,000 a year were uninsured.

Many Americans are uninsured for a number of reasons:

- they may be unemployed
- even if they are employed, their employer may not provide private health cover
- they do not qualify for Medicare (people over 65 years of age) or Medicaid (poor members of society), which are government-funded.

Who experiences inequalities?

- There are some 7.3 million children in the USA without health insurance – 9.8% of all children in the country.
- Ethnic minorities are far more likely to be uninsured than the American population as a whole. While just 13.9% of whites do not have insurance coverage, the same is true for 33% of Hispanics, 22% of blacks and 18% of Asians/Pacific Islanders.
- Perhaps as a result, despite notable progress in the overall health of the nation there are continuing disparities in the burden of illness and death experienced by minorities.

Government responses

The Affordable Care Act (ACA), known as 'Obamacare', was passed by Congress and signed into law by President Obama in March 2010. This Act gives people more health security by reducing the cost of medical insurance and improving the quality of healthcare. President Obama estimates the bill will cost $940 billion over a ten-year period from 2014.

Show your understanding

1 Explain the difference between the UK's NHS and the current health care system in the USA (before the introduction of the Affordable Care Act).
2 **(a)** What is health insurance?
  (b) Why do some people not have health insurance?
3 Who experiences inequalities in terms of their health?
4 Describe what the Affordable Care Act is.

Branch out

5 Do you think that American citizens should support the Affordable Care Act? Explain your answer.

Affordable Care Act (ACA)

In October 2013 the ACA, referred to by many as Obamacare, came into force despite strong opposition from the Republicans.

- Every state will have a health insurance exchange where people will shop for healthcare. Some states are running their own exchange while others are letting the federal government handle that task.
- Insurers must accept all applicants and cannot charge sick people more.

- To ensure the insurance companies can make a profit, all Americans, especially the young and healthy, must take out health insurance. From January 2014 those who refuse to take out health insurance will be fined.
- Those who are on low incomes will receive a government subsidy towards their insurance payment.
- It will move the country towards universal coverage, and will hopefully reduce health inequalities and keep costs down.

Crime and justice

When we consider the population of ethnic minorities in the USA and compare it with the prison population, there appears to be a link. Many argue that for ethnic minorities, especially blacks, involvement in criminal activity is connected to their ethnic group.

Figure 2.22 The Federal Correctional Institution in California

Why are there inequalities?

Most crimes that are committed in the USA take place in inner-city areas. These ghettos tend to be highly concentrated in poorer areas that are dominated by blacks and Hispanics. It is often suggested and argued that discrimination plays a big part when it comes to sentencing ethnic minorities at all stages of the justice system, such as:

- on arrest
- when being tried in court
- in terms of prison sentences
- the use of the death penalty.

Who experiences inequalities?

Black and Hispanic prisoners are generally younger and imprisoned at higher rates than white prisoners. In 2011 about 61% of the sentenced prison population was aged 39 or younger. More than half (52%) of white male prisoners were age 39 or younger, compared to 63% of black and 68% of Hispanic male prisoners.

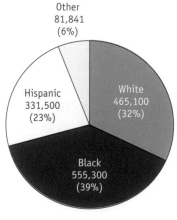

Figure 2.23 Estimated percentages of different ethnic groups among sentenced prisoners under state and federal jurisdiction, 2011

Source: Bureau of Justice Statistics

Race	Population	%
Black	1319	41.93
Latino	390	12.40
White	1358	43.17
Other	79	2.50

Table 2.1 Current US death row population by race, October 2012

ICT task

Go to www.deathpenaltyinfo.org and write down a list of the states that still use the death penalty to punish criminals.

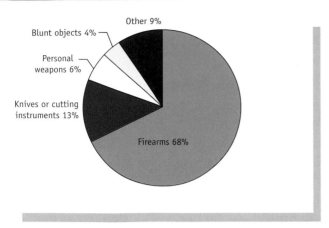

Figure 2.24 Murder weapons, 2011

Source: FBI, Get The Data

 Show your understanding

1 Explain why some ethnic minorities may experience inequalities in terms of the US crime and justice system.
2 Write down the number of people from each ethnic group who are on death row.
3 What is the most common murder weapon used in the USA?
4 Do you believe that America should abolish the death penalty? Write a paragraph that outlines your main reasons.

Gun crime

The USA has the highest **gun ownership** rate in the world: there are 89 guns for every 100 Americans, compared to just 6 in England and Wales. In Scotland, the calculated rate of registered firearms per 100 population is 4 as of 2012.

- In the USA in 2011, there were 12,664 murders, 8,583 of which were caused by firearms.
- In 2012, California had 1,790 gun murders – the highest number across all states – and equivalent to 3.25 per 100,000 people in the state.

However, most gun owners are responsible and law-abiding, and they use their guns safely. Many Americans believe strongly that the 2nd Amendment guarantees an individual right to bear arms (see page 11 for the Bill of Rights).

Thousands of innocent Americans are killed by gun violence each year. Over the past few decades there has been a rise in **mass shootings** that have shocked America and the world.

Government responses

In May 2013 President Obama unveiled a package of proposals to deal with gun violence in response to the Sandy Hook Elementary School shootings (page 26).

'Our nation has suffered too much at the hands of dangerous people who use guns to commit horrific acts of violence. We won't be able to stop every violent act, but if there is even one thing that we can do to prevent any of these events, we have a deep obligation, all of us, to try.' (*President Barack Obama*)

Another proposal, put forward as an amendment to the current gun bill, aimed to expand background checks to include online and unlicensed gun dealers. Fifty-four senators backed the plan, but that was six short of the 60-vote hurdle needed to clear the chamber so the proposal was rejected. President Obama lashed out at senators who blocked the plan: 'This was a pretty shameful day for Washington. But this effort is not over.'

The rate of people killed by guns in the USA is 19.5 times higher than similar high-income countries in the world. Between 1982 and 2012, the USA mourned at least 61 mass murders.

Case study: The Sandy Hook massacre

On Friday, 14 December 2012, one of the deadliest mass shootings in America happened at Sandy Hook Elementary School in Connecticut. It left 27 people dead (20 children aged between 6 and 7, and 7 adults including the gunman).

Before the events at the school

Before driving to the school, Adam Lanza, aged 20, shot and killed his mother, Nancy Lanza. He then took three guns from the house, dressed in black army-style clothes and an olive-green utility vest, and made his way to Sandy Hook Elementary School.

Earlier in the year, the school's security system had been upgraded, which required visitors to be admitted only after visual identification by video monitor. As part of this system, the school doors were locked at 9.30 a.m. each day, after morning arrivals.

The shootings

At about 9.35 a.m., when Lanza arrived, the gunman used an assault weapon to literally shoot his way through the locked glass door at the front of the school. Principal Dawn Hochsprung, school psychologist Mary Sherlach and vice-principal Natalie Hammond were in a meeting with other members of staff when they heard gunshots. Leaving the room, they rushed to the source of the sounds and encountered Lanza, who shot and killed Hochsprung and Sherlach. Hammond ran back to the meeting room and pressed her body against the door to keep it shut, but Lanza shot her through the door in her leg and arm.

Students heard shots across the school and described being ushered into washrooms and cupboards by the teachers after hearing the first shots.

Lanza then went into a first-grade classroom, where Lauren Rousseau, a substitute teacher, had herded her students to the back of the room. Rousseau and most of her students were killed, the sole survivor being a six-year-old girl who had 'played dead'. Lanza next went to another first-grade classroom, where Victoria Soto, the teacher, was killed, together with six of her students who had hidden under desks. Eleven children from Soto's class survived.

At the police station, the first emergency call about the shooting came in at 'approximately' 9.30 a.m. Police and other first responders arrived on scene about 20 minutes after the first calls.

Lanza stopped shooting between 9.46 a.m. and 9.49 a.m. after firing 154 rounds with the rifle. After realising he had been spotted by a pair of police officers who had entered the building, he fled from their sight before fatally shooting himself in the head with a handgun.

Figure 2.25 Mourners light candles during a vigil following the Sandy Hook shootings

- Stronger background checks – anyone who buys a gun would have to go through a criminal background check beforehand
- Toughen the background-check system by offering states $20 million in new incentives to share their information
- Ban on assault weapons – Obama is seeking to reinstate an earlier federal ban, which expired in 2004
- Limit high-capacity ammunition magazines – to slow down a shooter planning a massacre
- Get rid of armour-piercing bullets – although it is already illegal to manufacture and import these into the USA, the president wishes to ban their possession
- Prevent gun-trafficking – this measure would make it easier for the police to go after people who buy guns for other people and transfer them across state lines
- Review current laws that outline which people are prohibited from buying guns and make appropriate recommendations to improve the system

Figure 2.26 Obama's gun proposals

 ### Show your understanding

1 Explain what the US Government is doing to reduce gun violence.

Find out more

2 Find out about other mass shootings in the USA.
3 Write a paragraph that outlines your views on gun violence. Include recent examples and state whether you believe that Americans should have the right to bear arms.

Branch out

4 Take time to read the article on Senator Kelly Ayotte's views on gun control legislation (**http://tinyurl.com/bndr9pj**). Think about your views and opinions on Obama's gun control legislation.

 ## Added value

'Because of the rise of gun violence, America must vote in favour of tighter gun restrictions.' Investigate this statement and provide evidence to enhance your research. You may wish to provide examples of gun violence and arguments for and against gun control.

Family structures

Family life is very much part of the traditional image of life in the USA. In recent years in the West there has been change in family structure and a **breakdown** of the traditional **family unit**. Among the African-American population in the USA, there has been a greater breakdown of family structure: over 80% of children in ghetto areas are born into single-parent families.

By race and ethnic group, the share of the whole population who had ever married was similar for whites, blacks and Hispanics in 1960, but the decline in marriage has been particularly severe for African-Americans. By 2010 only 55% of black adults had ever married, compared with 64% of Hispanics and 76% of whites.

Why are there inequalities?

As the single parent is usually the mother, children grow up without an adult male as a role model. This can be particularly serious for boys who tend to follow older boys in their neighbourhood, often

	Blacks	Hispanics
Number of family households (millions)	9.4	10.7
Family households that are married couples (%)	44	63
Married-couple households that have children under the age of 18 (%)	38	61
Children living with two parents (%)	38	66
Family households with a single parent (mother) (%)	50	26
Single grandparents who live with their grandchildren under the age of 18. (Of this number, half were also responsible for their care.) (%)	17	14

Table 2.2 Hispanic and black family structures, 2011

Source: United States Census Bureau

getting involved in antisocial behaviour which leads to arrest by the police and dropping out of school. There is a growing dependency culture and not many males of working age actually work.

Single-mother poverty in the USA

Over one-quarter of US children under age 18 live with only one of their parents and as many as half of US children may live in a single-parent family at some point in their childhood. The vast majority – over 85% – of single parents are mothers.

Poverty is widespread and severe in **single-mother families**. According to the recently released Census Bureau data on poverty in 2010, people in single-mother families had a poverty rate of 42.2% and an extreme poverty rate of 21.6%. Poverty means an income of less than the official poverty standard, which was $14,570 for a family of two in 2010. Extreme poverty means an income of less than half the poverty standard.

Poverty rates are higher for single mothers who are women of colour. In 2010 the poverty rate was 50.3% for Hispanic single mothers, 47.1% for black single mothers and 32.7% for white single mothers. Three-fifths of poor single mothers were black or Hispanic. Two-thirds (66.8%) of poor single-mother

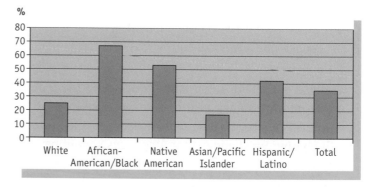

Figure 2.27 Children in single-parent families, 2011

families received food stamps in 2010, but only one-quarter (27.1%) received cash welfare assistance.

Obama's responses

Strengthen families

President Obama was raised by a single parent and knows the difficulties that young people face when their fathers are absent. He is committed to responsible fatherhood by supporting fathers who stand by their families and encouraging young men to work towards good jobs in promising career pathways. The president has also proposed an historic investment in providing home visits to low-income, first-time parents by trained professionals. The president and first lady are also committed to ensuring that children have nutritious meals to eat at home and at school, so that they grow up healthy and strong.

Promote work–family balance

Millions of women and men face the challenge of trying to balance the demands of their jobs and the needs of their families. Too often, caring for a child or an aging parent puts a strain on a career or even leads to job loss. President Obama believes we need flexible work policies, such as paid sick leave, so that working women and men do not have to choose between their jobs and meeting the needs of their families.

'The Task Force'

The American Recovery Reinvestment Act also boosts family incomes by expanding the child tax credit to cover an additional 10 million children in working families and creating a new Make Work Pay tax credit.

To help working mothers and fathers obtain quality childcare, the Act includes an additional $2 billion for the **Child Care and Development Block Grant**, $1 billion for **Head Start** and $1.1 billion for **Early Head Start**.

> The **Child Care Development Block Grant** is federal funding that provides assistance to childcare programmes and families. The funds will be used by states to provide vouchers to families for childcare or to provide access to care through childcare centres.
>
> **Head Start** is a programme that promotes the school readiness of children from birth to age five from low-income families by enhancing their brain, social and emotional development.
>
> **Early Head Start** is a federally funded community-based programme for low-income families with pregnant women, infants and toddlers up to the age of three.

Income and poverty

In 2011 the official poverty rate was 15.0%. There were 46.2 million people in poverty.

- In 2013 more than 19 million whites fell below the poverty line for a family of four, accounting for more than 41% of the nation's destitute.

Show your understanding

1. Explain the difference in family structure in America today compared to the past.
2. Compare family structures between different ethnic groups, focusing on single-parent families.
3. Read the text on single-mother poverty in the USA. Explain why these families struggle financially.
4. What schemes has the government introduced to try to help families financially?

Develop your skills

5. 'Black children are most likely to live in single-parent families. However, Hispanics have the lowest number of married couples.' (*Rachael McKay*).

Using Table 2.2 and Figure 2.27, give one reason to support and one reason to oppose the views of Rachael McKay.

- The number of Hispanics in poverty in 2011 was 13.2 million.
- For blacks, the 2011 poverty rate was 27.6%, which represents 10.9 million people in poverty.
- For Asians/Pacific Islanders, the 2011 poverty rate was 12.3%, which represents 2.0 million people in poverty.

Figure 2.28 In 2011 extreme poverty – meaning households living on less than $2 per day before government benefits – was double 1996 levels

About 39% are in what Americans would describe as the middle class, with annual earnings ranging between $35,000 and $100,000. The National Minimum Wage is $7.25 per hour and some states pay more than this.

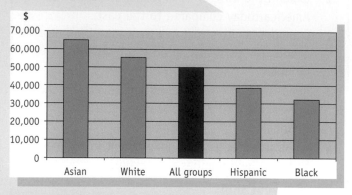

Figure 2.29 Average yearly household income by ethnic group, 2012

Source: US Census Bureau

Why are there inequalities?

In the USA there are a number of factors that contribute to the differences in wages observed between white Americans and Americans of other races:

- **Education**: this affects wages because it allows access to occupations of higher status that offer greater earnings.
- **Types of jobs**: whites and Asian/Pacific Islanders, who have the highest median incomes, are concentrated more in professional, executive and managerial occupations than blacks, Hispanics or American Indians.
- **Born outside the USA**: people who are not born in the USA but come to seek work are marginally worse off than other groups. Language barriers can cause difficulties for some immigrants trying to find work.
- **Discrimination**: research has found wage and employment discrimination against blacks, Native Americans, Hispanics and Asians/Pacific Islanders; however, discrimination has been found to be a much larger contributing factor for the wages of blacks/African-Americans than for wages of other races.

Who experiences inequalities?

Wage gaps have been identified for many races within the USA. However, research has found that the size and causes of the wage gap differs by race. Ethnic minorities in the USA tend to experience inequalities in terms of their income and prospects more than whites.

Government responses

The economic crisis has hit low-income American families particularly hard. President Obama has promised to help vulnerable Americans through this crisis by making sure they have the resources they need to put food on the table and keep a roof over their heads, while also extending tax credits to low-wage workers.

The **American Recovery and Reinvestment Act** included broad investments to alleviate the poverty made worse by the economic crisis. To fight hunger, the Act includes a $20 billion increase for the Supplemental Nutrition Assistance Program (SNAP), formerly known as food stamps. The Act provides increased income support, including an increase of $25 per week for unemployment insurance recipients and incentives for states to expand unemployment insurance eligibility, as well as an extra $250 payment to social security and supplemental security income beneficiaries and new resources for the Temporary Assistance for Needy Families (TANF) programme.

The rise of Asian/Pacific Islander Americans

Asian/Pacific Islander Americans are the highest-income, best-educated and fastest-growing racial group in the USA. They are more satisfied than the general public with their lives, finances and the direction of the country, and they place more value than other Americans on marriage, parenthood, hard work and career success, according to a comprehensive new nationwide survey by the Pew Research Center.

A century ago, most Asian/Pacific Islander Americans were low-skilled and low-wage labourers who were targets of discrimination. Today, they are the most likely of any major racial or ethnic group in America to live in mixed neighbourhoods and to marry across racial lines. When medical school graduate Priscilla Chan married Facebook founder Mark Zuckerberg in 2012, she joined the 37% of all recent Asian-American brides to wed a non-Asian groom.

Nearly three-quarters (74%) of Asian-American adults were born abroad. Of these, about half say they speak English very well and half say they do not.

Educational attainment is extremely important: more than six-in-ten (61%) adults aged 25 to 64 who have come from Asia in recent years have at least a bachelor's degree.

Figure 2.30 Asians recently passed Hispanics as the largest group of new immigrants to the USA

Employment

The 2008–11 recession was longer and more widespread than any recession since the Great Depression of the 1930s and the unemployment rate reached 10% in 2009. Since January 2012, the US economy has created 1.7 million jobs, but over 13 million Americans remain unemployed. In 2013, the unemployment figure is still above 8%.

Why are there inequalities?

There are several reasons for inequalities in employment, including:

- recession
- discrimination
- illegal immigration
- language barriers
- lack of skills and qualifications.

Who experiences inequalities?

Unemployment rates among the major race and ethnic groups remained high in 2010 as the US economy continued to slowly recover from the recession.

Blacks and Hispanics have suffered greatly from unemployment during this period and they for the most part have yet to rebound. Blacks are experiencing 16% unemployment and the figure for Hispanic/Latinos is around 12.5%. Those rates are drastically higher than the 8.7% unemployment rate for whites and 7.5% for Asians.

Government responses

President Obama believes this is a make-or-break moment for the middle class and those trying to reach it. He has laid out a blueprint for an economy that is built to last – an economy built on American manufacturing, American energy, skills for American workers and a renewal of American values.

The president signed the **American Recovery and Reinvestment Act**, which has been responsible for about 3 million American jobs and brought the economy back from the brink of another depression.

The president signed **Wall Street Reform**, the most sweeping reforms since the Great Depression, to hold Wall Street accountable, put an end to bailouts and the 'too big to fail' culture, enforcing the strongest consumer protections in history.

The president also signed the **Small Business Jobs Act**, which provides tax breaks and better access to credit for millions of small businesses.

Show your understanding

1   Compare the different incomes between the main ethnic groups (Figure 2.29). Are you surprised by the figures? Explain your answer.
2   Why do some ethnic minorities have a lower income than whites?
3   Provide evidence to prove that Asian/Pacific Islanders are the success story of ethnic minorities.
4   Give some reasons to explain why ethnic minorities may be unemployed.
5   How has the recession affected unemployment in the USA?
6   Compare unemployment figures for the main ethnic groups.
7   What is the government doing to try to create more jobs for American citizens?

Group presentation

8   In groups, look at one of the following factors to identify social and economic inequalities in the USA:
   • education
   • housing
   • health
   • crime and justice
   • family structures
   • income and poverty
   • unemployment.

   Your task involves the following:
   (a) Work together in your own group.
   (b) Make up a study aide for your chosen factor.
   (c) Think of inequalities that exist and of progress that has been made in that area.
   (d) Each group member should have a specific role, for example researching inequalities.
   (e) You can use a variety of sources such as books, notes and the Internet to research your topic.
   (f) Your teacher will collate your findings and photocopy a class set of them. You will then all have excellent notes for all of the main factors to help you with your understanding and revision.

Chapter 3

The Republic of South Africa

South Africa as a regional superpower and its relevance to Scotland

What you will learn:

1 Why South Africa is called the 'rainbow nation'.
2 Why South Africa is a regional superpower.
3 Why South Africa is relevant to Scotland.

The 'rainbow nation'

South Africa is a nation reborn. In 1994 the country elected its first multiracial democratic government after the end of white rule under a system known as **apartheid**. Nelson Mandela, the leader of the African National Congress (ANC), won the general election and became president. Until then, the white South African Government had denied the non-whites their political, social and economic rights. This has left a legacy of vast inequalities between the races, which still exists today.

After Mandela's election, Archbishop Desmond Tutu described post-apartheid South Africa as the 'rainbow nation'. In his first month of office, Mandela elaborated on Archbishop Tutu's words: 'Each of us is as intimately attached to the soil of this beautiful country as are the famous jacaranda trees of Pretoria and the mimosa trees of the bushveld – a rainbow nation at peace with itself and the world.'

The country has 11 recognised languages and, since the end of apartheid, progress has been made in making South Africa a more prosperous country for all. An elite group of black South Africans are now very wealthy, but many who live in the shanty towns (informal settlements) and poor rural communities have seen little change. South Africa is experiencing rapid urbanisation and 63% of its population now live in urban areas. Over one-third of the population are under the age of 15 and this, according to the current president, Jacob Zuma, has

The Afrikaans word **apartheid** means 'the state of being apart'. It describes the racial segregation that took place in South Africa between 1948 and 1994. This system affected all aspects of life. Numerous laws were passed to enforce segregation, such as the Group Areas Act of 1950 (which determined where people must live according to their race) and the Bantu Education Act of 1953 (which created a separate system of education for African students).

created 'a crisis of youth unemployment', with 51% of black South Africans aged between 15 and 24 without a job.

The apartheid years: 1948–94

It is important to have an understanding of the vast inequalities between the races created during the apartheid years as its legacy still exists in part today in South Africa.

The apartheid system was set up by the white group known as **Afrikaners**, whose ancestors came mostly from the Netherlands. In 1948 they gained control of the country from the English-speaking whites and set up a government that denied all non-whites their political, social and economic rights. Black people made up 70% of the population but they were given only 13% of the land area to live in; for example, the largest tribe, the Zulu, were

Nelson Mandela

Nelson Mandela was often described as 'the father of the nation'. His struggle to end apartheid, leading to 27 years in prison, explains why he was adored and respected by his people, who often referred to him as *Tata* ('father') and by his clan name, *Madiba*.

In 1994 he became the first elected president of the new South Africa, preaching conciliation between the races and working hard to create a new rainbow nation. Mandela retired from government in 1999.

He died on 5 December 2013 and the 'rainbow nation' mourned. President Zuma stated 'our nation has lost its greatest son'.

Figure 3.1
Nelson Mandela

to live in the homeland of KwaZulu-Natal and run their own affairs from there. The black population were treated as foreigners and had to have permission to live outside their homelands. They had to live in segregated areas in white South Africa called **townships** – the most famous of which was Soweto on the outskirts of Johannesburg.

In the late 1980s, the escalation of black unrest and international action against the white government of South Africa persuaded President F. W. de Klerk, leader of the National Party, that he must negotiate with Nelson Mandela, the imprisoned leader of the ANC. In 1990 Nelson Mandela was set free and the ANC declared legal. Prolonged negotiations took place and, finally, in 1994 a new constitution was agreed and elections were held. For the first time the black population could vote and Nelson Mandela and the ANC formed the new government. All the political parties agreed to the setting up of a **Truth and Reconciliation Commission (TRC)** to investigate illegal actions that had taken place during the apartheid years (see page 35).

The land and the people

South Africa is the most southern country in the continent and it has the most developed economy in southern Africa. It is five times the size of the UK with a population of 50 million. Because of its size, it has different climates and landscapes in different parts of the country. Much of the west of the country is desert, whereas the south, in the area around Cape Town, has a Mediterranean climate. South Africa is divided into nine provinces (see Figure 3.4).

Its population is made up of numerous ethnic groups and this is reflected in the recognition of 11 official languages. Black South Africans make up almost 80% of the population.

Figure 3.2 Racial segregation in action

The Truth and Reconciliation Commission

The Truth and Reconciliation Commission (TRC), chaired by retired Archbishop Desmond Tutu, was set up to establish as complete a picture as possible of the 'causes, nature and extent of the gross violations of human rights committed between 1960 and 1994'. The TRC had the power to grant an amnesty to anyone whose crime had a political purpose as long as they admitted their wrongdoing. Victims of apartheid had the opportunity to share their grief with the nation and to discover what had happened to their loved ones. The main hearings, aired on television, shocked and horrified the nation. The revelations damaged the National Party and led to the resignation of F. W. de Klerk. In total, 6,000 people applied for amnesty and 22,000 victims testified.

 Show your understanding

Branch out

1 Watch the 2004 film *Red Dust* starring Hilary Swank. In the film, the TRC visits a town to consider the amnesty application of a former white police officer and to investigate the death of a black activist during the apartheid years. It offers an outstanding insight into the brutality of the apartheid years and the segregation of the races that still exists in some areas today.

WWW

For further information on South Africa's Truth and Reconciliation Commission, go to www.justice.gov.za/trc

Ethnic groupings

South Africa is made up of four ethnic groups.

- The dominant group is the black population who are sub-divided by tribal group. The two main tribal groups are Xhosa (former presidents Nelson Mandela and Thabo Mbeki) and Zulu (current president Jacob Zuma).
- Whites are divided into English-speaking and Afrikaans-speaking.
- Coloureds are mixed race and most live in the Northern and Western Cape provinces.
- Asians (or Indians) are descended from Indian workers who were brought from India to work, especially in Natal, in the nineteenth century.

Table 3.1 indicates that South Africa's population is now just over 50 million. In 2009 the coloured population overtook the white population – an estimated 800,000 whites have left South Africa since 1994. With a higher birth rate than the other races, the black population has increased by more than 8 million since 1996 and it has now reached 80% of the population. In 2012 the white and coloured populations both stood at about 8.7% of the total, whereas Asians made up just 2.5%.

Provinces

South Africa is divided into nine **provinces**, each with their own parliaments and executives. Each province runs its own affairs but must abide by national government laws and policies. Eight of the nine provinces are controlled by the ANC. The one exception is the Western Cape, which is controlled

Figure 3.3 South Africa's population of 50 million is made up of numerous ethnic groups

Figure 3.4 South Africa's provinces

Ethnic grouping	1996		2012	
	Number (millions)	%	Number (millions)	%
Black	31.3	76.8	40.0	80.0
White	4.7	11.4	4.4	8.6
Coloured	3.3	9.0	4.5	8.7
Asian/Indian	1.2	2.8	1.3	2.5
Total	**40.5**	**100**	**50.2**	**100**

Table 3.1 South Africa's population

Source: Statistics South Africa, mid-year population estimates

by the Democratic Alliance (DA); it is the only province in which black South Africans are not the majority (see Table 3.2). The largest population group in the Western Cape is the coloureds and they number just over 3 million.

Provinces differ greatly in terms of size, population and wealth. Northern Cape is the largest in size but it has the smallest population. By contrast, Gauteng, which includes Johannesburg, is the smallest in size but it has the largest population. KwaZulu-Natal province is home of the Zulu king and has the second largest population. Western Cape and Gauteng are the wealthiest provinces and there are wealth, health and educational inequalities between these provinces and the poorest areas of Limpopo, Eastern Cape and Mpumalanga.

Illegal immigrants

Official figures detailing South Africa's population fail to include the millions of Africans who have flocked to the country to escape poverty and persecution in their home nations. It has been estimated by the South African Institute of Race Relations that over 4 million immigrants are living in South Africa. Most refugees originate from the Democratic Republic of Congo, Rwanda, Mozambique and Zimbabwe.

Province	Black total	White total	Coloured total	Asian/ Indian total	Total
Limpopo	5,148,000	93,000	14,000	9,000	5,264,000
Northern Cape	678,000	84,000	394,000	2,000	1,158,000
Western Cape	1,668,000	807,000	3,068,000	23,000	5,566,000

Table 3.2 Population groupings for selected provinces, 2013

Source: Statistics South Africa, Mid-Year Population Estimates

Province	Population (millions)
Gauteng	10.9
KwaZulu-Natal	10.6
Eastern Cape	6.6
Western Cape	5.6
Limpopo	5.3
Mpumalanga	3.7
North West	3.5
Free State	2.9
Northern Cape	1.2
Total	**50.3**

Table 3.3 South African provinces by population, 2012

Source: Statistics South Africa, Mid-Year Population Estimates

South Africa as a regional superpower

South Africa is a member of the G20 (see pages 1–2) and the only representative from Africa (Saudi Arabia represents the countries of the Middle East). Its importance was further demonstrated when South Africa joined the BRIC group, which represented the emerging economies of Brazil, Russia, India and China, to form the **BRICS**. The Fifth BRICS Summit was held on 27 March 2013 in the South African city of Durban.

South Africa is the regional superpower in southern Africa (see Table 3.4). It accounts for 85% of southern Africa's energy consumption and 90% of its gross domestic product (GDP). It is also the wealthiest country in sub-Saharan Africa in terms of natural manufacturing industry, as well as being the world's largest producer of gold. In 2012 it sent peace-keeping troops to the Central African Republic.

South Africa is the only country from Africa to have hosted the football World Cup finals, which took place in 2010.

Country	Population (millions)	GDP per head ($)	GDP (billions of $)
Mozambique	23.4	940	9.6
South Africa	50.5	10,570	363.9
Tanzania	45.0	1,430	22.9
Zambia	13.3	1,560	16.2
Zimbabwe	12.6	440	7.5

Table 3.4 South Africa as a regional economic superpower

Source: Adapted from *The Economist: Pocket World in Figures*, 2013

South Africa's relevance to Scotland

South Africa is a member of the **British Commonwealth** and was once part of the British Empire. However, the country was most upset when the UK Government announced in May 2013 that it was ending its annual £19 million aid package in 2015.

Scottish immigrants settled in South Africa from the eighteenth century onwards and there are strong ties between Scotland and South Africa. Scotland played its part in the international campaign to end apartheid. Glasgow was the first city in the world to make Nelson Mandela a Freeman of the City in 1981 – while he was still in prison – and it also changed one of its street names to Nelson Mandela Place. In 1993 Nelson Mandela finally came to Glasgow to receive his award.

South Africa can be seen as being both a developed country (such as Scotland) as well as a developing country in rural areas. It shares many of Scotland's problems such as wealth and health inequalities.

Social and economic issues

What you will learn:

1 The social and economic issues that exist in South Africa.
2 Government reaction and responses to social and economic issues.

With the end of apartheid, the passing of political control to the black majority was easy to achieve and the ANC has ruled the country with large majorities since 1994. Much more difficult was the removal of the social and economic inequalities between the races. In 1994 the ANC promised 'a job, a decent home and a chicken in every pot'. Some 20 years on, many South Africans are still

Show your understanding

1 Describe the inequalities that non-whites faced during the apartheid years.
2 What impact did the Truth and Reconciliation Commission have on the South African people?
3 Why is South Africa a regional superpower and why is this relevant to the people of Scotland?

Branch out

4 In pairs, create an information sheet on South Africa. You should include regional importance, ethnic groupings, population trends and reference to the nine provinces. Go to the South Africa Yearbook website at www.gcis.gov.za/content/resourcecentre/sa-info/yearbook for further information.

Develop your skills

5 'All of South Africa's population groups have witnessed an increase since 1994 and the province with the largest population is Gauteng.' (*Joseph Sisalu*)

Using Tables 3.1 and 3.3, give one reason to support and one reason to oppose the view of Joseph Sisalu.

waiting for this to be achieved. In this section we will examine the economic issues of employment and wealth and the social issues of education, health, housing and crime.

Wealth and employment

The South African Government uses **affirmative action** (known as **positive discrimination** in the UK) to favour non-whites in terms of employment, the allocation of government contracts and entry to higher education. This is regarded as necessary in order to redress the decades of discrimination by whites against the black population. As such, all employers are compelled by law to employ previously disadvantaged groups, such as blacks, coloureds and Indians.

However, appointments are not based on merit but on racial quotas, which whites argue is unfair. Many whites argue that reverse racism now exists.

These laws have accelerated the appointment of educated non-whites to the top posts in universities and the civil, police and health services, and led to the creation of wealthy black business people. Critics of the scheme argue that it has helped only a small group of blacks while the majority have seen no benefit. Black unemployment is officially 25% of the total population, but the actual figure is estimated to be nearer 40%.

FACT FILE

Affirmative action legislation

- **Employment Equity Act**: any firm with more than 50 employees must ensure that their organisation represents the population balance of 75% black and can be fined up to £100,000 if it does not meet these terms. All central and local government departments adhere to this Act.

- **(Broad-Based) Black Economic Empowerment (BEE) Act**: the BEE directorate monitors the progress made in appointing blacks to senior posts in universities, the legal profession and private firms. No government contracts will be awarded to firms that fail to have the approved racial quotas in their workforce. Entry to universities, for example, must reflect these racial quotas and not be based simply on exam results.

'**Black Diamonds**' are part of a new elite group of over 3 million blacks that now have top jobs in government or business. They live in the wealthiest suburbs of South Africa's cities beside their white neighbours. Their children go to the best state schools or to private schools, and they have private health insurance to ensure the best medical treatment. Many, such as the ANC businessman Cyril Ramaphosa, are millionaires. All this suggests that the wealth divide is not so much based on race but on social class.

Widening wealth inequalities

Former President Thabo Mbeki referred to South Africa as being a land of two nations: one white

and rich, and one black and poor. For a non-white living in a township with only basic amenities, a high crime rate and poverty, this statement is true. For the educated, prosperous black middle classes, this statement reflects the past as they live in their wealthy suburbs and drive their top-of-the-range cars: '**Black Transformation**' is a reality. South Africa is a country where the wealth gap between the rich (the white and the new black elite) and the poor – including unskilled whites – is widening (see Table 3.5). About 10% of whites, mostly from the Afrikaner community who were once guaranteed employment in central and local government, experience poverty.

Officially, unemployment is 25% in South Africa but the accepted figure is 40%, with youth unemployment even higher. Social grants have played a critical role in ensuring that the poor are not left in dire poverty. In 1999, 2.5 million people benefited from grants. By 2009 this figure had risen to over 13 million. The social grants system is the largest form of government support for the poor. Most is given in the form of child support, which reached 7.8 million families in 2007 compared to only 34,000 in 1999. It is not surprising that many blacks are willing to challenge their low wages and take to the streets, as was the case in Marikana in 2012 (see page 48).

The **Gini index** (see Table 3.5) measures the extent of wealth inequalities within a country, where 0 corresponds with perfect equality (where everyone has the same income) and 1 corresponds with perfect inequality (where one group has most of the income and everyone else has little income).

Country	1991	2011
Brazil	0.53	0.52
China	0.25	0.44
South Africa	0.55	0.69

Table 3.5 Gini index (wealth inequality), selected countries, 1991 and 2011

39

Figure 3.5 A 'Black Diamond', one of South Africa's new black elite

Education

Massive inequalities existed in education provision between the races. The ANC governments need an educated black workforce to raise living standards and to take up the top posts in industry, commerce and professions such as lawyers, doctors and teachers. Affirmative action and other legislation have been passed, which effectively discriminate against whites in order to accelerate black social and economic progress and prosperity (see page 39). However, there is still a shortage of skilled and highly educated black South Africans while an abundance of poorly educated, unskilled black South Africans face a lifetime of formal unemployment.

Since 1994 progress has been made to improve the quality of learning for black students: separate schooling for the different races has now ended, exam results have improved (see Figure 3.6), the number of schools with no electricity or modern facilities has declined significantly and now more blacks go to university than whites. This has been achieved with the government investing 21% of its entire spending budget in education, and spending on education doubled between 2006 and 2012. Free education has been expanded to enable students in poor urban and rural areas to attend school – this figure has increased from 0.7% in 2002 to 55% in 2011 – and these students also receive a nutritional lunch referred to as a 'Mandela sandwich'.

Major improvements have also taken place in further and higher education. Black South Africans now make up more than 65% of university and further education students. All higher education must meet racial quotas to ensure that African students are not under-represented. White students claim that they are being discriminated against as many African students receive entry despite having inferior exam results. The rejected white students can take no action as the Constitution provides for whites to be discriminated against in order to achieve 'Black Transformation'.

However, many claim that education is failing the 12.6 million learners enrolled in the education system. In the *World Economic Forum Global Competitiveness Report*, South Africa ranks 132nd out of 144 countries for its primary education and 143rd for the quality of its science and maths.

Province	1996	2010
Eastern Cape	21.0	12.0
Guateng	9.5	4.4
Limpopo	36.9	17.0
Mpumalanga	29.4	15.0
Western Cape	6.7	2.9

Table 3.6 Percentage of children who do not attend school in selected provinces, 1996 and 2010

The **Institute for Justice and Reconciliation (IJR)** stated that nearly 80% of high schools are failing their children and that the overwhelming majority of children in the failing schools are black Africans. The IJR also stated that 'the best schools are those that were reserved exclusively for white children prior to 1994 and these schools today should enrol the poorest children'. The IJR argued that the 400 Dinaledi schools should be expanded as these schools were on the way to excellence. The Dinaledi project is a partnership between state schools and the business sector, with the emphasis on maths and science.

The South African Government is investing in modernising schools. Figure 3.7 highlights the improvements that have been made, but much has still to be done.

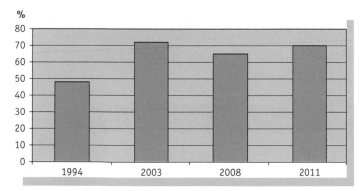

Figure 3.6 Percentage pass rate for grade 12 matriculation senior certificate

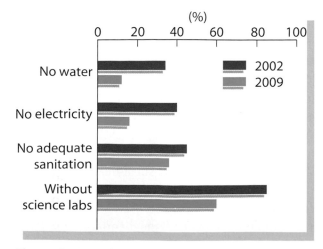

Figure 3.7 The infrastructure of schools

Province	Pass rate (%)
Eastern Cape	58.1
Gauteng	81.1
KwaZulu-Natal	77.2
Western Cape	82.9

Table 3.7 Selected provincial matriculation results, 2011–12

FACT FILE

Progress in education

- In 2012 the South African Government invested 21% of the entire budget in education (6% of GNP).

- Spending on education doubled between 2006 and 2012.

- Progress has been made in reducing the number of schools with no sanitation, water or electricity. This number has been reduced to less than 40% today.

- Black South Africans now make up 65% of students in higher education.

- Grade 12 matriculation results (equivalent to Scottish Higher) have improved significantly. In 1996 the pass rate was 48.9%; by 2011 it had risen to about 70%.

- Free education has been expanded to enable students in poor urban and rural areas to attend school. The figure has increased from 0.7% in 2002 to 55% in 2011. These same students receive a nutritional lunch ('Mandela sandwich').

- The number of adults with literacy problems has decreased. The Kha Ri Gude Mass Literacy Campaign was launched in February 2008, with the intention of enabling 4.7 million South Africans to become literate and numerate in one of the 11 official languages by 2012.

- The percentage of adults over the age of 20 who have reading problems has declined from 27% in 2002 to 18% in 2012.

- Quotas are used to ensure entry to higher education for non-white students. They address the disadvantages that many black children face in their schooling.

Widening education inequalities

Substantial inequalities exist between the provinces in terms of provision. In the Western Cape, 96% of schools have electricity, whereas in the Eastern Cape only 40% of schools have this provision. Substantial inequalities exist between the provinces in terms of exam results. In Gauteng, for example, the pass rate is over 80% whereas in Limpopo the figure is 58%.

There is a massive skills shortage, with industry finding it difficult to find staff, yet there are millions of unskilled, semi-literate unemployed workers. Schools in the poorest (black) communities suffer teacher shortages, overcrowding and buildings with no electricity or sanitation and only basic resources. Schools with the poorest results are the all-black schools in the townships or rural communities, whereas schools with the best results are the former all-white schools or private schools with a mixture of students from all races. In short, segregated education still exists through location and poverty.

Health

Under presidents Thabo Mbeki and Jacob Zuma, significant progress has been made in improving **primary health care** in both rural and urban areas. Around 3,600 primary health clinics have been built and more than 700 mobile clinics set up, providing basic health care in the most remote areas. Twelve state-of-the-art hospitals have been built to tackle the poor hospital facilities available in provinces such as the Eastern Cape. Immunisation against tuberculosis, whooping cough, diphtheria, polio and measles is available free of charge to all children under the age of six.

Some 40% of all South Africans live in poverty and 75% of these live in rural areas where health services are least developed. Regional inequalities reflect the urban–rural divide. Gauteng and the Western Cape are highly urbanised and have the best health provision (see Table 3.8). Malnutrition is a major problem in rural areas alongside

Figure 3.8 Inequality is still a problem in South Africa's school system

Show your understanding

1 What is the purpose of affirmative action legislation?
2 To what extent has it improved the living standards of the black population?
3 **(a)** Who are the 'Black Diamonds'?
   (b) Describe their lifestyle.
4 Why is it not correct to say all whites are rich and all blacks are poor in South Africa?
5 Describe the improvements that have been made in education. You should refer to government spending, exam results, entry to further and higher education, and improvement to school buildings.
6 What evidence suggests that education inequalities still exist?
7 'The quality of schooling is substandard, especially in the township schools.' (*Trevor Manuel*)
   To what extent is Trevor Manuel correct?

outbreaks of cholera in KwaZulu-Natal and tuberculosis in Eastern Cape. Since 1996 a key weapon against ill health and disease has been the availability of a clean water supply. Over the last 18 years, 12 million South Africans have been provided with a clean water supply. As with other things, regional inequalities still exist in the percentage of households with no toilet. Child mortality rates double when there is no access to clean water.

Projects such as the **National Primary School Nutritional Project** for needy school pupils have improved health standards as well as attendance at school. Every day about 6 million children in over 18,000 schools munch on a 'Mandela sandwich'. For those not covered by medical aid schemes, free health care is provided. South Africans' use of health services has doubled over the last ten years and 8% of GNP is spent on health provision.

Province	Doctors
Eastern Cape	13.0
Gauteng	35.5
Mpumalanga	11.0
Western Cape	37.5

Table 3.8 Doctors per 100,000 of the population by selected province, 2012

Source: SA Health Statistics

There is a strong private health service, which inevitably reflects a racial imbalance in favour of whites and ensures that they have access to better health provision. However, the growing number of 'Black Diamonds' (see page 39) means that over 8 million people have private cover but that leaves 42 million depending on an over-stretched national health service.

HIV/AIDS

Unfortunately, all government efforts to improve the health of black South Africans have been undermined by the scourge of HIV/AIDS. The statistics in Table 3.9

illustrate the devastation of HIV/AIDS, with life expectancies still lower than in 1994. The strain placed on health services, the economy and social services is immense: it is estimated that there are 1.5 million HIV/AIDS orphans.

President Thabo Mbeki was slow to react to the crisis when he came to power in 1999. He initially refused to give free anti-AIDS drugs to all HIV-positive pregnant women and their children and only began to do so after he was ordered by the Constitutional Court to provide the drugs free of charge to mother and child at birth.

FACT FILE

The AIDS pandemic
- Over 60,000 children aged between one month and five years die each year.
- In 2007, at its peak, 700 South Africans died every day from AIDS.
- 6 million South Africans, mostly blacks, have the disease.
- Over 1 million children under the age of 18 have lost their mothers to AIDS.

The **2012 National HIV Survey** indicated that KwaZulu-Natal, Mpumalanga and Free State have the highest HIV prevalence and that, among the races, black Africans had the highest HIV rate. According to government figures, 5.7 million South Africans suffer from HIV/AIDS and it is women in their late 20s who are the hardest hit.

The resignation of President Mbeki in December 2007 led to greater urgency in tackling the AIDS crisis through treatment and prevention. President Zuma has ensured free treatment for HIV-positive babies and pregnant women, and over 1.5 million South Africans now receive anti-AIDS drugs. The success of these actions is reflected in the increase of life expectancy from 54 years in 2005 to 59 years in 2011 and also a significant decrease in infant and under five mortality.

Gender and race	HIV prevalence (%)
Male	8.2
Female	13.3
Black	13.3
White	0.6
Coloured and Indian	2.9

Table 3.9 Estimated figures for HIV prevalence among South Africans by gender and race

Show your understanding

1 Outline the progress made in health care provision in recent years.
2 Why is HIV/AIDS a major problem in South Africa?
3 In what ways has President Zuma reduced the impact of HIV/AIDS?

Nkosi Johnson

Figure 3.9 Nkosi Johnson

'I want people to understand AIDS – to be careful and respect AIDS. You can't get AIDS if you touch, hug or hold hands with someone who is infected. Care for us, and accept us. We are all human beings, we are normal. We have needs just like everyone else. Don't be afraid of us. I just wish the government would give anti-AIDS drugs to all HIV-positive pregnant women and their children.'

These are the words of 11-year-old Nkosi Johnson at an international AIDS conference held in Durban in South Africa in July 2000. Nkosi had been born HIV-positive and had been abandoned by his mother. He was sent to a hospice to die. There, he was adopted by a white woman, Gail Johnson, and so he outlived both his parents (who died of AIDS). However, within a year of the conference Nkosi was dead. Such was the impact he had made on the world community that his death was mourned across the globe.

ICT task

Working in pairs, use the Internet to create a slide presentation explaining who Nkosi Johnson was and the impact he had around the world.

Housing

The wealth divide in South Africa is reflected in the segregated housing patterns in the towns and cities of South Africa. Although the new 'Black Diamonds' live in the former white areas in their gated mansions and communities, the vast majority of blacks live in formal traditional black townships and those who are unemployed or who have moved in from the countryside live in informal settlements (squatter camps), devoid of electricity and modern sanitation. **Soweto** is an example of a formal township that can now boast modern homes with electricity, a shopping mall and up-market housing.

Since 1994 the government has built over 4 million homes. Between 1998 and 2011, the number of black property owners increased by 80%. According to the 2011 census, 85% of households have access to electricity and nine out of ten homes have access to water.

The **National Water and Sanitation Programme** has brought clean water to over 9 million (mainly rural) homes. Unfortunately, a culture of non-payment of rents and amenities charges still persists. The situation has not been helped by the privatisation of services, which has led to an increase in charges. The government provides 6,000 litres of water per household per month free of charge to more than two-thirds of South Africa's population.

Households using electricity	1996 (%)	2001 (%)	2010 (%)
For lighting	58	70	84
For cooking	47	51	69
For heating	45	49	60

Table 3.10 Access to basic services, 1996–2010

Source: South African household survey, 2013

Land reform

Land reform, especially in the countryside, is a major issue. A new **Department of Land Affairs** was created in 1994, with responsibility for developing and implementing a policy of land reform.

Townships and informal settlements

Figure 3.10 An informal settlement

Great progress has been made to improve the quality of housing in secure dwellings in townships by providing electricity and water supplies and internal sanitation (see Table 3.10). However, millions of non-whites live in insecure dwellings with no electricity or running water. They are the people trapped in poverty, with poor health and surrounded by crime. Unemployment is over 50% and many have poor literacy skills. Schooling is basic: many of the children do not complete secondary school and do not have the skills to contribute to or benefit from the government initiatives. Gauteng and North West provinces have the largest number of informal settlements. The social grants they receive from the government keep them afloat (see page 39). Many of these settlements are a result of the move from the countryside to the towns and mining areas. Some of the employees who worked in the Marikana diamond mine lived in such informal settlements (see page 48).

The plan involved:

- compensating those who had lost their land because of apartheid laws
- setting up the Land Reform Programme to assist rural workers to manage their own land
- giving tenants the right to buy the land they farm and protection from eviction.

The original **Reconstruction and Development Plan (RDP)** promise of redistribution of 30% of agricultural land within five years was totally unrealistic. Black ownership of land has increased from 13% in 1994 to 20% in 2012. The government has been successful in providing compensation to the many blacks who chose financial payments rather than allocation of land. Therefore, this partly explains the limited increase in black land ownership. By 2010, 75,500 land cases costing 4.4 billion South African rand had been settled by the **Chief Land Claims Commission**.

The **'willing buyer–willing seller'** principle has been at the core of South Africa's land settlement, guaranteeing that land will be acquired by the state at fair prices and given to the landless blacks. The government has the power to force a compulsory sale if a white farmer rejects the original offer.

Crime

The fear and impact of crime is one issue that unites all races. Although many whites and rich black Africans seek safety in their walled estates, ordinary black and coloured South Africans protect their families as best they can. The availability of guns is a major problem: anyone can buy an AK47 rifle in any taxi queue for about £30. On average, 44 murders take place *every day*. Of these, 26 are caused by guns.

Crime in South Africa is high because of the following reasons:

- The apartheid years created a **culture** of violence in South Africa and there is easy access to guns. The

association of law enforcement and the rule of law with the apartheid regime have created a lack of respect for the police within the black community, even though only 12% of the force is white.

- The vast **inequalities** in terms of wealth in South Africa have created a 'war' between the 'haves' and the 'have nots'.
- Massive **influxes** of poor people from the countryside to the towns and the arrival of illegal immigrants (estimated at 4 million) from other African countries have created a group in society that ignores its laws.

Official government figures clearly indicate that South Africa is a less violent country than previously. The number of murders has declined by 35% since 1994 – the official 2012 figure is 16,900 per year. However, this still represents 44 murders a day, making South Africa one of the most dangerous places to live.

The Democratic Alliance (DA) argues that many crimes are not reported as the public have little faith in the culprits being caught. Crimes of rape and aggravated robbery at residential premises have increased and this explains the fear factor experienced by South African citizens. South Africa has one of the highest rates of sexual violence in the world and the reported figure in 2012 was 64,000 cases.

Fear of white farmers

Afrikaner farmers and their families are concerned about their safety in the isolated communities in which they live. Since 1994 over 3,000 farmers and their families have been murdered and more than 10,000 attacked. In April 2010 Eugene Terreblanche, the controversial leader of the extreme Afrikaner group the AWB, was murdered on his farm by two of his black workers.

Case study: South Africa's culture of violence and Oscar Pistorious

In February 2013 Oscar Pistorius, the world-famous South African paralympic athlete, shot dead his girlfriend. This he does not deny, but he blames the culture of violence for his actions. He was afraid that there was an intruder in his apartment and that, at best, he might be robbed and badly beaten up and, at worse, murdered, as dead bodies tell no tales. On iMaverick, a South African website, the headline was *Just Another South African Story*. In short, Pistorius blames the culture of fear and distrust especially among whites that in an unequal and racially divided society you fire first and ask questions later.

Pistorius and his girlfriend were staying in a luxury gated community in Cape Town surrounded by electric fences and high walls, and with 24/7 security – yet he still did not feel safe. The wife of the last white president of South Africa, F. W. de Klerk, was shot dead in such a well-protected gated community.

South Africans do not trust the police. The last two police commissioners were sacked for corruption and, in 2012, 30 Durban police officers – all members of an elite police organised crime unit – were suspended

Figure 3.11 Oscar Pistorious

and accused of 28 murders and 100 other offences.

For wealthier whites and non-whites, protection comes from private security firms and life in gated communities such as the one in which Pistorious was staying. For the majority of blacks in the townships and informal settlements, local vigilante groups dispense their own punishments to criminals, ranging from beatings to killings.

South Africa has the 10th highest murder rate in the world and violence against women – especially rape – is widespread.

ICT task

Working in pairs, use the Internet to investigate the case of Oscar Pistorius.

Police and crime

The disclosure that the lead police officer investigating the murder of Pistorious's girlfriend was himself accused of the death of citizens, and the world-wide coverage of police dragging a suspect on the ground into their police van, has once again placed the limitations and corruption of the police in the public spotlight.

In 2009 President Zuma promised tough action against criminals to ensure a peaceful 2010 World Cup and this was achieved. He appointed Bheki Cele as national police commissioner. Cele replaced Jackie Selebi, who was charged with taking bribes. The new commissioner promised to shake up the police and root out corruption. However, he himself was dismissed in 2012 by Zuma after allegations of corruption. Selebi was jailed for 15 years for talking bribes.

Case study: The Marikana massacre

On the afternoon of 16 August 2012, members of an elite special unit of the South African police force opened fire on a group of striking miners at Lonmin mine, a platinum mine near Marikana, North West province. On this day 34 people were killed and at least 78 were injured. The incident was the single most lethal use of force by South African security forces against civilians since the apartheid era.

Video footage from different angles shows that the police were pushing the strikers into a small area. Groups of strikers began singing protest songs and marched along police lines. The police fired tear gas and rubber bullets into these groups.

The South African police service said that the miners had refused a request to disarm and attacked them with various weapons, including firearms taken from the two police officers killed earlier in the week. South Africa's police commissioner claimed that the 500-strong police force was attacked by armed strikers, stating, 'The militant group stormed toward the police, firing shots and wielding dangerous weapons.'

A month after the shootings, President Zuma said that 'we regarded the incident of Marikana as an unfortunate one. Nobody expected such an event'. Archbishop Desmond Tutu called the Marikana massacre 'a nightmare for South Africa' and attacked the corruption of ANC leaders (see page 54).

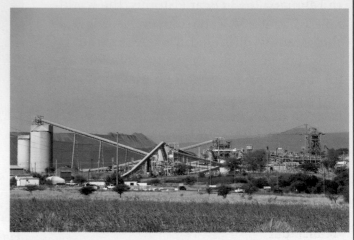

Figure 3.12 The Marikana mine where 34 striking miners were killed by police

In the light of these events, the Marikana Commission of Inquiry was appointed by the president to investigate matters of public, national and international concern arising out of the shootings.

In September 2013 the judge in charge of the public inquiry halted the hearings. He accused the police of lying about what had happened. New evidence had emerged of a group of miners being chased to a nearby hill and being killed in cold blood. Photographs came to light showing some of the dead miners on the ground without weapons at their sides; in the police photographs they were holding weapons.

ICT task

Working in pairs, use the Internet to investigate the findings of the inquiry into the Marikana massacre.

Show your understanding

1 Describe the improvements made in the provision of housing and basic services.
2 Why has little changed for those who live in informal settlements?
3 Describe the South African Government's policy on land reform.
4 Why does Oscar Pistorius blame South Africa's culture of violence for the death of his girlfriend?
5 Why did Archbishop Desmond Tutu call the Marikana massacre 'a nightmare for South Africa'?

Branch out

6 Working in pairs, draw a mind map outlining why crime is so high in South Africa.

Political issues

What you will learn:

1 The political system of South Africa and its democratic features.
2 The main political parties and election results.
3 To what extent South Africa is a successful democracy.

South Africa's political system

South Africa is regarded as a democracy since the end of apartheid in 1994. Most South Africans are proud of their written constitution, which provides a wide range of rights to its citizens and outlines the powers, structures and limitations of government and parliament. However, many whites are unhappy with Article 9.2 of the Constitution, which discriminates against whites. The Constitutional Court made up of senior judges can declare the government's actions illegal in order to protect the rights of its citizens. Citizens can participate in elections at national, provincial and local level and have a wide range of parties to choose from (see Table 3.12 on page 52). A free press exists and citizens can criticise the actions of the government, join a pressure group and/or a trade union such as the National Union of Miners (NUM).

Yet some fear that the dominance of the African National Congress (ANC) and the corrupt activities of some of its members are turning the country into a one-party state, where criticism of the government is seen as white racism or, if by blacks, as a betrayal of fellow Africans. Jacob Zuma's comment in 2008 that 'the ANC will rule South Africa until Jesus returns' horrified many South Africans for its arrogance.

National government

Although South Africa has on paper a federal system of government, the reality is that the central government totally dominates the provinces. Only in the Western Cape is there an alternative to ANC rule; in 2009 the Democratic Alliance (DA) gained overall control of the province. The political structure is illustrated in Figure 3.13.

The executive

The **executive** is made up of the **president** and his **cabinet**. The president is elected by the **National Assembly** from among its members. The ANC dominates elections and so the leader of the ANC is always chosen as president (see Table 3.11). He is the executive head of state and leads the cabinet. The president may not serve more than two five-year terms in office. The cabinet consists of the president, the deputy president and 25 ministers. The president appoints the deputy president and ministers, and may dismiss them.

President	Term of office
Nelson Mandela	1994–99
Thabo Mbeki	2000–08 (forced to resign)
Kgaleme Motlanthe	2008–09
Jacob Zuma	2009–present

Table 3.11 Presidents and terms of office

The judiciary

South Africa has an **independent judiciary**, which acts as the guardian of the Constitution. The highest court of the land is the Constitutional Court, which has 11 judges including the chief justice. They are appointed for life and when there is a vacancy the president appoints a replacement. One of the most recent decisions of the Constitutional Court was to uphold the right of South African citizens living abroad to vote in the 2009 general election. Concern exists that Jacob Zuma, under the slogan of 'Black Transformation', is trying to undermine the independence of the Constitutional Court by criticising its white judges. Further concern was raised when Zuma stated, in a pre-election address in 2009, that judges were not gods.

The legislature

South Africa has a **bicameral** (two-chamber) parliament consisting of a **National Assembly** (400 members) and a **National Council of Provinces (NCOP)**. The NCOP consists of 90 delegates (10 from each province) and 10 delegates representing local government.

Elections for both houses are held every five years based on a system of proportional representation. However, this means that voters do not elect their representative and cannot vote him out of office at the next election. MPs' loyalty is with their leader.

Bills amending the Constitution require a two-thirds majority in the National Assembly as well as a supporting vote of six out of the nine provinces represented in the NCOP.

Central government

Provincial government

All nine provinces have their own legislature and government led by a premier. In 2009 eight of the nine premiers were appointed by Jacob Zuma. This ensures that the ANC leadership controls the provincial parties and weakens the powers of the provincial governments. Provincial governments are expected to deliver policies decided by the national government. Several have been heavily criticised for their mismanagement of education and health resources.

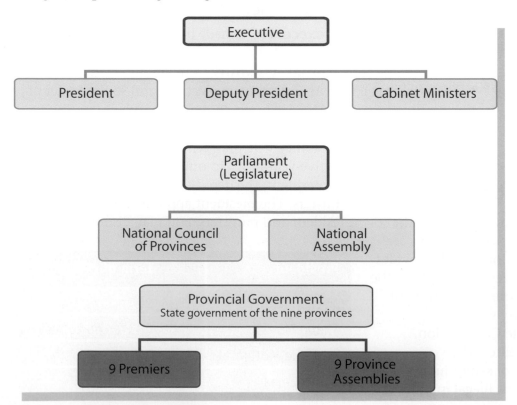

Figure 3.13 Central government

Local government

There are 283 local councils, referred to as **municipalities**, and large cities such as Cape Town and Johannesburg have their own metropolitan municipalities. Many mayors of these municipalities are failing to deliver basic services, partly because of mismanagement and corruption (see page 54). Most local councils are controlled by the ANC, but in Cape Town citizens have used the ballot box to elect the main opposition party, the Democratic Alliance (DA), to run the city.

IS THE ANC LOSING ITS GRIP ON SOUTH AFRICA?

Mr Booysens is the new major of Bitou, a township in Western Cape province. He has done what was once unthinkable for a black South African: resigned from the ANC and joined the Democratic Alliance. He stated: 'when we took over the municipality in the 2011 local elections it was shocking — the municipality was insolvent. It was corrupt from top to bottom.' The previous Mayor had leased a top of the range BMW, which upset many as they saw it as one more example of the ruling ANC elite flaunting their new wealth.

Adapted from news sources

The main political parties and elections

General (national) elections take place every five years using a closed-list, **proportional representation** system known as the **national list**, where the percentage of votes cast for a political party closely matches the percentage of seats won by the party. The voters do not vote for a particular candidate but for a party. This ensures strict party loyalty as the party leader can remove a candidate from the list. It also encourages the formation of new parties: in 2008–09 supporters of Thabo Mbeki left the ANC and formed the Congress

of the People (COPE) and in 2013 Mamphela Ramphele announced the formation of Agang, a new political party. New parties divide and weaken the opposition to the ANC.

A further concern has been a **decline in registration** and **voting turnout**, although turnout was higher in the 2009 election with the emergence of COPE. Although turnout in South Africa is significantly higher than turnout in the UK, it is clear that a sizeable number of South Africans are disillusioned that the promises made in 1994 have not been delivered and they see no point in registering their vote. Many Africans do not choose to vote for the ANC based on its policies or record; instead, they base their support on their loyalty to the party of liberation and Nelson Mandela.

The 2009 election

The 2009 election result was a personal triumph for Jacob Zuma and the ANC. Corruption charges against Zuma had been thrown out and his supporters had forced President Mbeki to resign in 2008. Mbeki's supporters announced the formation of a breakaway party, the Congress of the People (COPE), led by former ANC ministers. However, the leaders of COPE had limited funds to fight the election and were too closely associated with the discredited Mbeki. The party gained only 30 seats in the National Assembly.

Figure 3.14 Jacob Zuma, leader of the ANC and South Africa's president

Party	Description
African National Congress (ANC)	The ANC dominates South African politics and is the party of Nelson Mandela and the black majority. It has won all four general elections and is expected to do so again in 2014. Its leader is Jacob Zuma, who is also the president of South Africa.
Democratic Alliance (DA)	This party replaced the New National Party (NNP) as the official opposition party in the 2004 elections and has increased its support at every general election. It gained control of the Western Cape after the 2009 elections. Its main supporters are whites, people of mixed race and Asians/Indians, and its leader is Helen Zille.
Inkatha Freedom Party (IFP)	The IFP, led by Chief Buthelezi, draws its support largely from Zulu-speaking South Africans and supports greater powers for the provincial governments. It is a party in decline, losing heavily to the ANC in the 2009 elections in KwaZulu-Natal.
Congress of the People (COPE)	This new political party was formed in 2008 by former Xhosa members of the ANC who had supported Thabo Mbeki. It came third in the 2009 elections, but failed to win enough black support to challenge the ANC.

Table 3.12 Main political parties in South Africa

The result was an overwhelming victory for the ANC, which won almost 66% of the vote. Its greatest triumph was in KwaZulu-Natal, where Jacob Zuma, a Zulu, used his Zulu heritage against the Inkatha Freedom Party (IFP). The ANC, however, failed to retain control of the Western Cape provincial government.

The DA further increased its support to 17% of the national vote and achieved an outstanding victory in the Western Cape. Its leader, Helen Zille, continually reminded voters of past allegations of corruption against Zuma and denounced the ANC as presiding over a 'failed state'. The DA had widened its racial support from whites to embrace the coloured and Asian/Indian communities of the Western Cape. The results in the Western Cape reflect that voting in South Africa is based on race (see Desmond Tutu, p.55). Although blacks account for almost 80% of the whole population, they comprise only 30% of the population of the Western Cape. Helen Zille declared that 'the Western Cape is leading South Africa towards democracy.'

The IFP continued to suffer heavy electoral losses. For a party that dominated KwaZulu-Natal from 1994 to 2004, it endured the humiliation of being routed by the ANC. In 1994 the IFP received 1.8 million votes in KwaZulu-Natal; in 2009 the party received only 780,000.

Party	Seats			Votes		
	1999	2004	2009	1999 (%)	2004 (%)	2009 (%)
African National Congress (ANC)	266	279	264	66.3	69.9	65.9
Democratic Alliance (DA)	38	50	67	9.6	12.6	16.7
Inkatha Freedom Party (IFP)	34	28	18	8.6	6.9	4.5
Congress of the People (COPE)	–	–	30	–	–	7.4

Table 3.13 National Assembly election results for the main political parties, 1999, 2004 and 2009

Province	ANC (%)	DA (%)	IFP (%)	COPE (%)
Eastern Cape	68.8	9.9	0.1	13.6
Gauteng	64.4	21.9	1.5	7.8
KwaZulu-Natal	62.9	9.1	22.4	1.3
Limpopo	84.8	3.4	0.1	7.5
Western Cape	31.5	51.4	0.1	7.5

Table 3.14 Voting support for selected provinces, 2009 elections

Figure 3.15 Helen Zille, leader of the DA

Party	Seats in 2004	Seats in 2009
ANC	19	14
DA	12	22
Independent Democrats	3	2

Table 3.15 Western Cape provincial election results, 2009

Jacob Zuma

The president of South Africa is a controversial figure. For some he represents the unacceptable face of democracy, a man accused of massive corruption and of a lavish lifestyle, supporting his six wives and 20 children. The latest outcry is the planned £14 million expansion to his lavish rural homestead to include a helicopter pad, parking for 40 vehicles and houses for three of his wives. On the other hand, his humble rural background and lack of formal education make him highly popular among the majority of blacks who are poor. He is a '100% Zulu boy' who offers hope to those who live in poverty.

Corruption

Every country has its corrupt politicians and the dominance of the ANC in every walk of life inevitably provides opportunities for politicians and officials to enrich themselves. Standards of public auditing are abysmal and every year huge sums of public money are stolen.

In 2010 the **Special Investigating Unit (SIU)**, South Africa's anti-corruption body, said it had identified 400,000 civil servants getting welfare payments to which they were not entitled. Many leading ANC leaders have been found guilty of corruption, including Tony Yengeni, chief whip of the ANC, and Winnie Madikizela-Mandela, former wife of Nelson Mandela. President Zuma has promised to root out corruption, but he himself had been accused of taking bribes from foreign firms when he was deputy president. His financial adviser was found guilty and Zuma's case was dismissed only on political grounds.

WWW

For further information on SIU, go to www.siu.org.za

Further controversy arose in 2013 when it was discovered that his state-of-the-art ranch mansion being built in Nkandle, KwaZulu-Natal, was costing the taxpayer R328 million. The most recent trial for corruption has been that of the former chief of police and a senior ANC figure, Jackie Selebi. According to the South African *Sunday Times*, 'Selebi may also be the country's most powerful gangster'. In January 2010 the wife of the minister of state security, Siyabonga Cwele, was arrested and charged with drug-trafficking.

In 2012 **Transparency International** ranked South Africa as the fourth-cleanest state of Africa's 53 countries and 56th out of the 180 countries it judges worldwide. So it can be argued that South Africa has an excellent record of tackling corruption and is ranked well above most other African countries by corruption monitors.

WWW

For further information on the work of Transparency International, go to www.transparency.org

Tenders milk the state dry

In 2012 the Special Investigating Unit (SIU) stated that the Department of Public Works (DPW) had come to resemble a cesspool of corruption, with public officials being bribed to give contracts to particular firms. The SIU discovered that public officials regularly awarded **tenders** to individuals in exchange for financial benefits. In one instance, two officials received R4 million in return for awarding a R320 million contract to the successful bidder. Contracts are routinely awarded for services never delivered and the money is shared between officials and the corrupt firm.

'I have over the years voted for the ANC, but I would very sadly not be able to vote for them after the way things have gone. We really need a change. The ANC were very good at leading us in the struggle to be free from oppression. They were a good freedom-fighting unit. But it doesn't seem to me now that a freedom-fighting unit can easily make the transition to becoming a political party. Very many people are really voting with their hearts, rather than with their heads. Emotionally, you need a real turnaround to get them to see that when you vote for a political party you are voting for its policies and whether those are the things you want to see happen. It is no longer something that you can base on emotional links we had with the people who strove for our freedom.' (*Desmond Tutu, May 2013*)

Show your understanding

1 Describe the political rights of all South Africans.
2 Outline the main features of the South African political system.
3 Why does the ANC dominate South African politics?
4 Outline the evidence which suggests that political corruption is a problem in South Africa.

Develop your skills

5 'The 2009 general election was a triumph for the ANC in both the national and provincial elections and a disaster for the DA and IFP.' (*Jacob Zuma*)

Using Tables 3.13 to 3.15, to what extent does the evidence support the above statement?

Tendering is when private firms are invited to put in a bid to win a contract. In theory, the lowest bidder who meets the standards is awarded the contract.

The media

South Africa has a thriving free and independent press, with liberal newspapers such as the *Mail & Guardian* keeping a close and critical watch on the actions of the government. However, the government intends to pass a **Protection of Information** bill that would limit the freedom of the press to expose ANC corruption.

Television plays an important role in maintaining the culture and languages of South Africa. The impartiality and independence of the South African Broadcasting Corporation (SABC) is an issue of major debate in South Africa. Tony Leon, a prominent South African politician, has accused the SABC of 'becoming a virtual propaganda arm' of the ANC. COPE also complained that the SABC failed to provide live coverage of its final rally before the 2009 elections, and refused to accept that it had been a technical fault.

Theoretical debate: discrimination against whites

Twenty years after the end of white rule, discrimination is an everyday occurrence in South Africa. **Affirmative action** is an important vehicle for creating black empowerment and redistribution of wealth between the races. However, white children born after May 1994 into the new multiracial democratic South Africa are discriminated against because of their colour. Can this be justified in a democratic society?

The Constitution makes clear reference to the need to address the inequalities created by apartheid. Article 9.2 states: 'To promote achievement of equality, legislative and other measures designed to protect or advance persons or categories of persons disadvantaged by unfair treatment may be taken.'

Show your understanding

Branch out

1   Working in pairs, create three arguments to support and three to oppose the view that South Africa is a successful democracy.

Class debate

2   Organise a class debate on the motion: 'Affirmative action is necessary in order to reduce inequalities between the races.'

I run my own company and provide badly needed employment for my fellow black Africans. It is only fair that I should be awarded government contracts to build schools and hospitals, which our people were denied for so long. I have a lifestyle that my father could only dream about. The ANC has no other choice if we wish to end the massive inequalities that exist in our society. Our leading figures in business, in education and in the civil service must be black.

Under apartheid, when I went for a job I was not white enough. Now I am told I am not black enough.

I can appreciate why it has to be done, but it is at the expense of our children's future. It is unfair that black Africans with inferior qualifications go to universities ahead of whites or get appointed to the top law firms with a poor degree.

Figure 3.16 Is affirmative action a fair policy?

To what extent is South Africa a successful democracy?

Arguments for

- South Africa is a stable model of democracy for Africa. There have been four peaceful elections based on proportional representation. Over 35 political parties participated in the 2009 elections, with 13 parties sitting in the National Assembly. The proportional representation system encourages the formation of new political parties.

- A peaceful transition from Mandela to Mbeki occurred. The power struggle between Mbeki and Zuma was resolved peacefully with the resignation of Mbeki as president in September 2008.

- South Africa has a federal system of government with powers divided between central and provincial governments. Local government structures provide local services. The Western Cape is controlled by the DA and this has prevented the ANC from totally dominating politics.

- South Africa has a liberal Constitution, guaranteeing freedom to all its citizens. It provides for an independent judiciary. The Constitutional Court ordered Mbeki to provide drugs to combat HIV/AIDS.

- There is a free press and civil society able to criticise and monitor the actions of the government. The success of the Truth and Reconciliation Commission highlights the openness of South African society.

Arguments against

- There is a fear that South Africa is becoming a one-party state. The ANC has won convincingly all four elections and controls eight of the nine provinces; only in the Western Cape is it in opposition. The ANC has 264 of the assembly seats. In contrast, the official opposition, the DA, has only 67 seats.

- There is an issue of corruption, with leading ANC members being sent to jail. President Zuma was under investigation for eight years over charges of corruption. The charges were dropped in April 2009 in controversial circumstances.

- Minority rights, such as Afrikaner and Zulu culture, are under threat. Zuma appoints all eight premiers of the provinces under ANC rule and there is lack of democracy within them. The people do not directly choose the president or premiers of the provinces.

- The policy of transformation politics could threaten the independence of judges and the rights of non-black South Africans. The South African Broadcasting Corporation (SABC) is regarded as being the mouthpiece of the ANC. Zuma could threaten the independence of the judiciary through new appointments to the Constitutional Court. Attempts were made in 2012 to limit the powers of the press.

Chapter 4

The People's Republic of China

China as a superpower and its relevance to Scotland

Geography

The People's Republic of China is the third largest country in the world in terms of land mass, after Russia and Canada. It covers an area of 9,596,962 km². From north to south, it stretches 5,500 km (3,400 miles) and from east to west 5,000 km (3,100 miles). It also has land borders with 14 other countries.

The sheer size and diversity of China's landscape and terrain has, in many respects, influenced its development. China also experiences a variety of climates: from deserts in the north-west to hot tropical rain forest in the south-west; from hot, humid summers on the south and east coast to cold, dry winters in the north-east.

The overall result is that most of the recent economic development in China has taken place in the eastern coastal provinces at the expense of the rural interior, which has been left more underdeveloped. This inequality is noticeable in the east-coast cities where skyscrapers and white-tiled buildings are commonplace, whereas moving west away from these cities the country gets more noticeably poorer with subsistence farming and high illiteracy.

People and culture

The People's Republic of China has a population of 1.33 billion. This is one-fifth of the whole world's population and more than any other country on Earth. Around one-third of these people live in urban areas or cities, with the rest living in more rural areas in the country. There are several ethnic groups in China. The largest of these is the Han Chinese, who make up about 91.5% of the total population. The remaining 8.5% are Zhuang, Manchu, Hui, Miao, Uyghur, Yi, Mongol, Tibetan, Buyi and Korean.

Is China a global superpower?

In this first quarter of the twenty-first century, an era of globalisation, the world is witnessing a shift from the dominance of the West, led by the USA and the European Union, to the rise of Asia, led by China.

Since the global recession of 2008, EU countries including the UK have been shaken by debt crises, defaults and bailouts. On the other hand, China has been one of the few countries unaffected by the global economic downturn, showing growth rates of around 10% consistently throughout the past several decades. In 2010 China became the world's second largest economy and it is expected to be the largest by 2016.

> **What you will learn:**
> 1 Why China may be considered to be a global superpower.
> 2 Why China is relevant to Scotland.
> 3 The impact of China on other countries.

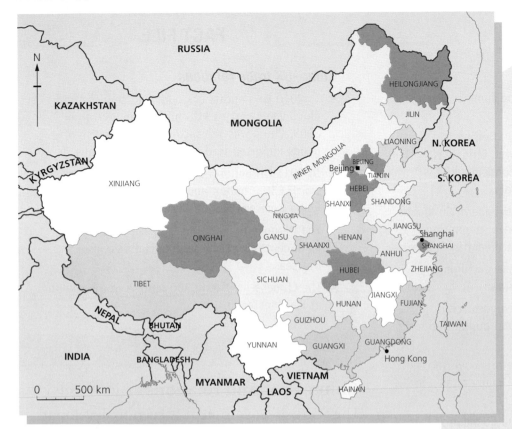

Figure 4.1 The People's Republic of China

Figure 4.2 China's flag is deeply symbolic

So could China be considered a global power? Militarily, China still lags behind the USA; for example, while the USA has eleven aircraft carriers, China has only one. Politically, its global influence is also limited and in terms of technology and living standards it lags far behind the USA. In fact, the only sense in which China is a superpower is economic: its economy is currently over half the size of the US economy and is projected to overtake it.

It is probably true to say that in time China will be a global superpower based on economic dominance. It is estimated that China's economic strength will be massive, far greater than that of the EU. Even at its present low level of development, China is already the main trading partner of many countries around the world, and with its economic power will also gain political power and influence.

China and international relationships

In support of its desire to promote a foreign policy of peace, China is playing an increasingly active role in **international affairs**. It has supported the international war against terrorism in the **United Nations Security Council** (where it holds one of the five permanent seats) and it voted in favour of limited sanctions on North Korea and Iran. However, China's support of Syria demonstrates its determination to protect its own interests.

China–EU relations

The EU is China's biggest trading partner and China is the EU's largest source of imports. The EU has benefited from the growth of the Chinese market and is committed to open trading relations with China. The total value of EU trade with China reached €433.8 billion in 2012. In 2010, the EU and China collaborated on foreign affairs, security and global challenges such as climate change and the recovery of the global economy.

Recent key events in China

- 2008 August: Beijing hosts the summer Olympic Games.

- 2010 January: the USA calls on Beijing to investigate cyber attacks, saying China has tightened censorship. China condemns US criticism of its Internet controls.

- 2010 October: jailed Chinese dissident Liu Xiaobo is awarded the Nobel Peace Prize, prompting official protests from the government in Beijing.

- 2011 July–August: police kill seven Uighurs (members of a Turkic ethnic group).

- 2012 January: official figures suggest city dwellers outnumber China's rural population for the first time.

- 2013 January: Nearly 100 Tibetans have set themselves on fire since 2009, many fatally, in protest at Chinese rule.

- 2013 March: vice-president and Communist Party chief Xi Jinping takes over as president. Li Keqiang takes over as second in command, the new premier.

- 2013 September: Jiang Jiemin, head of the body overseeing China's state-owned companies, is removed from his post on alleged corruption charges. This is one of several high-profile corruption investigations involving top leaders.

China–UK relations

The UK's relationship with China is seen by the government as a political and economic priority. In 2013 the Chancellor said it is important for Britain and China to take 'the next big step together…working together for both our benefit'. The UK wants to shape its economy towards manufacturing and exporting more overseas, while relying less on financial services.

For China, it's the opposite. It wants to shape its economy away from too much investment in manufacturing towards developing a more diversified service sector to provide for its burgeoning middle class.

China–UK trade relations

- In 2010 UK imports of goods and services from China were worth £31.8 billion, up 23% from 2009. China was the second largest source of goods imported into the UK, after Germany.

- In 2011 UK imports of goods from China were worth £30.2 billion and UK exported goods to China were worth £8.8 billion.

- The UK government aims to make London the main centre for Chinese financial business overseas.

- The Chinese invested £800 million in a new hub at Manchester Airport.

China–Scotland relations

The Scottish Government is keen to develop its relationship with China because China is an important export market for Scotland. There are currently many Scottish companies doing business in China, with great opportunities for more. For example, exports of whisky and salmon have witnessed a significant rise in demand.

Why China for Scotland?

The Scottish Government is keen to promote a relationship with China that will bring benefits to both countries. Scotland continues to offer support and assistance to China as it continues its economic and social reforms. It is looking to China to support and assist its economic recovery and future prosperity.

China's growth rate of 9.2% in 2011 is considered exceptional and China has contributed to a third of world growth. It is the world's largest goods exporter and importer. It offers trade opportunities for Scottish businesses and it hopes to attract Chinese investment in Scottish industry.

Why Scotland for China?

Despite differences in wealth, Scotland has much to offer China. To China, Scotland is a country that:

- is open for business and is an ideal destination for investment within the EU
- has a world respected reputation for hosting major sporting and cultural events like the Ryder Cup and the Edinburgh International Festival
- offers opportunities for joint projects in research and development, for example the Confucius partnership between Scottish and Chinese schools reflects warm relationships between the countries
- offers opportunities for cultural exchanges and sporting links along with tourism.

 Show your understanding

1 Describe in detail whether you think China could be considered to be a global superpower.
2 Describe China's international relationships.
3 Describe China's relationship with the EU and the UK.
4 Explain why China is important to Scotland.

Branch out

5 Create your own Fact File on China. Include sections on geography, people and culture, the Chinese flag and recent key events.

Political issues

What you will learn:

1 The role of the Chinese Communist Party in government and society.
2 What the main institutions of government are.
3 Levels of participation.
4 The extent to which China could be considered to be democratic.
5 The representation of citizens in the political system.

The Communist Party of China

For over 60 years China has been run by the **Communist Party of China (CPC)**. The CPC rules China strictly, and any opposition or criticism to its total control is met with brutal force. In 2012 the CPC had over 85 million members, making it the largest political party in the world. By comparison, in 2012 the UK Labour Party had around 193,000 members and the Conservative Party around 130,000.

The CPC is heavily involved in the lives of ordinary Chinese people. In every village there are local Party officials who keep an eye on everything going on. They monitor and influence what people learn at school, watch on television and access on the Internet, as well as all aspects of work and housing and even the number of children they have (see page 80).

Membership of the CPC

Being a party member means significant **privileges**, which is why membership is continuing to rise. Members can apply for jobs restricted to Party members and their children have access to better education and schools. However, it

FACT FILE

The Communist Party of China

- Date of establishment: July of 1921.
- Place of establishment: Shanghai, China.
- General secretary and president of the People's Republic of China: Xi Jinping.
- Motto: Seeking Truth From the Facts.
- Flag and emblem: the hammer and sickle design indicates the party is representing classes of workers and peasant.
- Guiding ideology: Marxism–Leninism and Mao Zedong Thought.
- Party membership: 85 million.
- Total number of branches: over 3.3 million grass-roots branches.

is not easy to join the CPC. When you are 18 you have to apply by writing a personal letter to your local party, be accepted into a study group, have your thinking and background thoroughly checked, then be approved as a probationer member. You also have to attend a formal joining ceremony before the party's flag and swear the party oath:

'It is my will to join the Communist Party of China, uphold the party's program, observe the provisions of the party constitution, fulfil a party member's

duties, carry out the party's decisions, strictly observe party discipline, guard party secrets, be loyal to the party, work hard, fight for communism throughout my life, be ready at all times to sacrifice my all for the party and the people, and never betray the party.'

> The ideology (political beliefs) of communism was based on the teachings of the German nineteenth-century political philosopher **Karl Marx**.

Mao Zedong

Figure 4.3 Mao Zedong

Mao Zedong's picture can still be found on public display all across China. He was born in 1893 into a peasant family in Hunan province, central China. After training as a teacher, he travelled to Beijing where he worked in the university library. It was during this time that he began to read the literature of **Karl Marx**. In 1921 he became a founder member of the Communist Party of China (CPC). He ruled China from 1949, when the communists gained power, until his death in 1976.

Mao set out to reshape Chinese society, using propaganda and force to shape the country in his own image. All banks, factories and utility services such as electricity came under state ownership

and China's farmers began to be organised into collectives. The upper classes were wiped out and all wealth was controlled by the people through the CPC. All opposition was ruthlessly suppressed and all aspects of life – religion, family values and political opinions – were controlled by the party.

In 1958, in an attempt to introduce a more 'Chinese' form of **communism**, Mao launched the Great Leap Forward. This involved the mass mobilisation of labour to improve agricultural and industrial production. However, the result was a massive decline in agricultural output which, together with poor harvests, led to famine and an estimated 6 million deaths. The policy was abandoned and Mao's position weakened.

In an attempt to re-assert his authority, Mao launched the Cultural Revolution in 1966, aiming to purge the country of 'impure' elements and revive the revolutionary spirit. One-and-a-half million people died and much of the country's cultural heritage was destroyed. In September 1967, with many cities on the verge of anarchy, Mao sent in the army to restore order. Mao appeared victorious, but his health was deteriorating. His later years saw attempts to build bridges with the USA, Japan and Europe.

When Mao died in 1976, the new leader Deng Xiaping introduced the system that exists today of a **socialist market economy**. Wealth and private ownership are now allowed, but vast social and economic inequalities exist. However, strict political control still remains.

The selection process is competitive. In 2012, 22 million people applied and only 3 million were accepted. It is no surprise then that Party members form an elite group that is unrepresentative of China's society. For example, fewer than 20% of Party members are female and nearly 80% of all members are over the age of 35. However, children get exposed to politics from the age of six, when they wear the red neckerchief of the Young Pioneers. Nevertheless, formal political education does not start until children join the Communist Youth League at the age of 14. China's president, Xi Jinping, and premier, Li Keqiang, both joined the CPC aged 21 and have never worked outside it.

Xi Jinping

Figure 4.4 Xi Jinping

Xi Jinping is the Communist Party chief as well as the president of the People's Republic of China. He is a so-called 'princeling', the privileged son of a former top leader. However, Xi's father, a top revolutionary leader, fell from grace in one of Mao Zedong's periodic purges. In 1968, 15-year-old Xi was sent to the countryside to learn from the peasants, hauling manure and coal.

Xi is China's first leader born after the 1949 Communist revolution. His father's purge hurt Xi's political standing as he was not admitted to the party until 1974, after 10 unsuccessful attempts. 'I did not lose heart and had no feelings of inferiority,' he said. 'I just thought that there were more good than bad people in the party.'

Xi has proven more assertive and unpredictable than many China watchers anticipated. Warning that corruption could bring down the party, he launched a campaign that has targeted senior officials and called for more open criticism of the government. He has also stressed the need to relaunch stalled economic reforms. Looking for a slogan to encapsulate his viewpoint, Xi has adopted the phrase 'Chinese Dream'. It is used to describe the aspiration of individual self-improvement in Chinese society.

Li Keqiang

Figure 4.5 Li Keqiang

Li Keqiang is current premier of the People's Republic of China, taking office in March 2013. He graduated from high school in 1974, during the Cultural Revolution (see page 62), and was sent for rural labour. He eventually joined the CPC and made his way in, becoming the party head of the local production team. He was awarded the honour of 'Outstanding Individual in the Study of Mao Zedong Thought' during this time.

Li became the youngest Chinese provincial governor in 1998. According to provincial officials working with him at the time, he refused to participate in any banquets or large fancy events not related to government activities.

He is known to be outspoken, and led economic development in Henan, transforming the poor inland region into an attractive area for investment. He trekked through all regions of the province trying to search for a comprehensive solution to its growing problems. He has also reiterated the importance of industrialisation, urbanisation and agricultural modernisation in China in order to improve its competitiveness, food security, energy security, affordable housing and health care.

China's other parties

China is sometimes considered to be a **one-party state**. However, there are alternative, non-communist, democratic parties to the CPC. For example, there are eight political parties other than the CPC, which are known collectively as the **United Front**. They include the:

- Revolutionary Committee of the Chinese Guomindang
- China Democratic League
- China Democratic National Construction Association.

These organisations are small and all accept in their constitutions the dominant position of the CPC. There are also a large number of social organisations in China all controlled by the CPC, of which the major ones are the All-China Federation of Trade Unions, the All-China Youth Federation, the All-China Women's Federation and the All-China Federation of Industry and Commerce.

The main institutions of government

- **Politburo**: the Politburo (the political bureau) has 24 members, almost all of whom are male. It is at the centre of all political decision-making in China. However, real power lies with its smaller standing committee, which works as a kind of inner cabinet. How the standing committee operates is secret and when a decision is made, all members are bound by it.

- **National People's Congress (NPC)**: this has around 3,000 members who, after election, remain in position for five years. Most members are also CPC members, so their loyalty is to the party first, the NPC second. It is the legislative branch or parliament of China's government, but it merely rubber stamps decisions made by the Politburo.

- **Central Military Affairs Commission (CMAC)**: this has 12 members who control the People's Liberation Army (PLA) and the paramilitary People's Armed Police. The chairman of the CMAC is also the general secretary of the CPC. It has always been the role of the military to protect the party, so China's PLA has always defended the party as much as its national borders. All PLA officers are also party members and they must make a declaration of loyalty to the party.

- **Discipline Commission**: this investigates and deals with corruption among party **cadres**.

- **Armed forces**: the People's Liberation Army (PLA) is seen as the defender of the CPC. Officers and men have to declare their loyalty

> **Cadres** are people who have been fully indoctrinated in party ideology and methods and are given leading roles at local level in administration and political education.

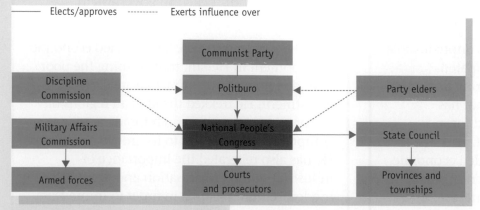

Elects/approves ········· Exerts influence over

Figure 4.6 How China is governed

When ousted leader Bo Xilai's case rocked China in 2012, it was the Discipline Commission that sealed his fate. Bo was removed from his post as Communist Party chief by the Politburo following the murder of a British businessman by his wife, to which he is linked. Bo was found guilty and imprisoned.

to the party and study its teachings. PLA officers are also party members, and there is a separate party machine inside the military to make sure rank and file stay in line with party thinking.

- **State council**: China's state council is responsible for implementing party policy from national to local level.

- **Provinces and townships**: there are four major tiers of government in China: national, provincial, protectorate and county. It has 22 provinces, 5 autonomous regions, 4 municipalities (considered so important they are under central government control) and 2 special administrative regions. Decisions are made at the top and flow downwards to the counties and into the cities and towns at the local level.

- **Special Administrative Regions (SARs)**: these were established in order to address the special circumstances concerning the two regions of Hong Kong and Macao. Hong Kong was a British colony that was returned to China in 1997. These issues are based on the concept of 'one country, two systems', where two completely different economic systems (socialist and capitalist) and ideologies can coexist.

ICT task

Go to the BBC website at www.bbc.co.uk/news/world-asia-pacific-13904437 and use the interactive flow chart explaining how China is governed. Remember to take notes as you do so.

CPC ENDORSE LIU ZHIJUN EXPULSION

The Communist Party of China (CPC) on Sunday endorsed a decision to expel former Railways Minister Liu Zhijun from the CPC. The decision was made by the Political Bureau of the CPC Central Committee. Liu was stripped of his CPC membership after he was found to be involved in corruption.

He was found to have used his influence to seek huge illegal profits for private businessmen, which caused great economic losses and negative social influence. The CPC Discipline Inspection also discovered Liu had taken massive bribes and bore the major responsibility for severe corruption in the railways system.

Liu's illegal gains have been confiscated and his case has been handed over for investigation to judicial authorities. Liu's removal is also believed to be linked to the high speed train collision of July 2012 that killed 40 passengers and injured 172 others, the tragedy having been blamed on improper management.

Adapted from news sources

Political participation

In China people have the opportunity to participate in the political process in many ways.

Standing as a candidate and campaigning

In 2012 a large number of Chinese sought to stand as candidates for seats in local people's congresses, the Chinese equivalent of a city or state assembly. Most were barred from even registering, waylaid by bureaucratic excuses and then threatened and harassed at home and work. Many had sought to publicise their campaigns online, but Beijing monitors the Internet relentlessly for political challenges (see page 80).

Voting in elections

- **Local congress**: in each province, people over the age of 18 can elect deputies for the local people's congress.

- **Village elections**: around 1 million villages hold village elections to elect village committees that can make decisions on local issues.

- **Hong Kong**: in 2012 Hong Kong voters had the opportunity to elect a new legislature, with pro-democracy candidates on the ballot paper. For the first time, 40 of the 70 seats on the governing legislative council were directly elected. However, under current laws, 30 of the 70 seats in the assembly were chosen by a small group of electors selected along economic and professional lines.

China's future leaders undergo no open competitive process because they are selected by a small circle of top officials whose decisions are later confirmed in nominal procedures. There are no elections in the general sense in China except at local level.

Becoming a member of the CPC and holding political office

See 'Standing as a candidate and campaigning' and 'Voting in elections' above.

Taking part in protests or demonstrations

Chinese citizens can take part in protests and demonstrations if they are approved by the Communist Party. However, criticism of the state is not tolerated.

Most of the Chinese public is far removed from the political process. The election of a new leader about every decade is done in a secretive decision-making process. For example, in 2012, more than 2,200 carefully vetted delegates attended the party congress. Their chief task was to select a central committee of about 200 members. That committee, in turn, chose the 25-member Politburo and its standing committee, although the positions are believed to have been decided in behind-the-scenes negotiations rather than in a direct vote.

In traditional Chinese culture, women are expected to care for their families after work. Since 1949, when the Chinese central government was established, no woman has ever entered the Politburo standing committee (the top governing body). In the current Politburo, out of the ruling party's top 25 leaders, only 2 are women. From a wider perspective, only 33 out of 205 members of the ruling Communist Party's Central Committee are women.

 Show your understanding

1 Describe the membership of the CPC compared to that of the UK's political parties.
2 Explain the selection process of the CPC.
3 Describe the main branches and bodies of the Chinese Government.
4 Describe two ways a person can participate in the political process in China.

Develop your skills

5 'Women in China are well represented in government.' (*Hu Wan*)
Explain why Hu Wan could be accused of exaggeration.

Social and economic issues

What you will learn:

1 The social and economic issues that exist in China.
2 Government reaction and responses to social and economic issues.

Migrant workers

More and more factories have been built in China, so the country has seen mass population transfer as tens of millions of migrant workers have left the countryside to find higher paid work in the cities. This, in turn, has created a new domestic retail environment, with greatly increased demand for **consumer products** further fuelling the development and growth of **urbanisation**. In 2005 there were two megacities of 10 million people or more; by 2025 this number is expected to have risen to eight.

Number of cities

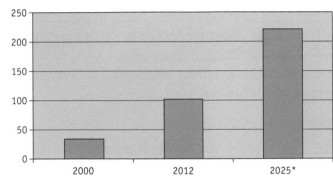

Figure 4.7 Number of cities in China of 1 million people or more

* Predicted

Who are migrant workers?

Migrant workers in China are people who work in places other than the towns of their household registration (**hukou**). The hukou is usually based on their place of birth or home village, and frequently migrants have not lived there for more than six months. After economic reforms in the late 1970s, migrant workers in China emerged as a social issue when millions began leaving their home villages in search of work.

China's migrant workers are the backbone of the country's labour force, working mainly in low paid jobs on construction sites and in factories. Historically, migrant workers have been seen as an important source of cheap labour. They are often willing to take the lowest paid, most dangerous jobs that others are unwilling to undertake. Approximately 210 million migrants work in Chinese manufacturing and construction industries, and the vast majority of these

Figure 4.8 A cramped dormitory for migrant workers in Beijing

are from rural areas. There is a large percentage of migrant workers in urban industries. For example, in Wuhan 43% of manufacturing workers and 56% of construction workers are migrants.

Government data indicates that there were 262 million migrant workers in 2013; in 1989, there were about 30 million. Chinese migrant workers are a big component of the Chinese **labour force**. They are primarily people from impoverished regions in rural and western areas who move to urban areas and crowd the more prosperous eastern and south-eastern coastal areas looking for work. The All-China Federation of Trade Unions' research shows that 77% of all manufacturing workers, 80% of all construction workers and 33% of all service workers are migrant workers.

According to the China National Bureau of Statistics, 45% of current migrant workers are employed in the manufacturing industry compared to 31% previously. Construction, which was traditionally the chosen sector of migrants, now has

> The **hukou** is the restrictive registration paper or residency permit that ties a migrant worker to their home town. This means they can receive benefits only back in their home town and not in the cities where they go for work. Migrants have little or no social security, including access to education for their children, health and other welfare provisions.

only 10% of migrant workers compared to 28% previously. In 2013 over 680 million people lived in cities – 52% of China's entire population of nearly 1.35 billion. With 75% of Chinese expected to be living in cities within 20 years, the demand for more jobs, transport, energy, water and other vital infrastructure is set to rise.

Workforce, wages and working conditions

When China embarked on a market-economy path 30 years ago, hundreds of millions of Chinese were added to the workforce. China's workforce today has around 815 million workers, but there are still hundreds of millions of rural Chinese peasants who are poised to join this workforce. Around 221 million Chinese workers are migrant workers who are usually farmers or people from rural areas going to cities and coastal areas to do jobs deemed too dangerous or dirty for urban residents.

The wages of migrant workers, in particular, have lagged far behind the national average: in 2011 their average wage was almost half that of the national average. A migrant worker earned around 2,000 yuan ($300) a month compared to the national average wage of 3,500 yuan ($525) a month.

Although the average monthly wage for workers in China has increased every year over the past decade, there remain substantial inequalities between different groups of workers, industrial sectors and geographical regions. Many factory workers are migrants from the countryside, who work an average of 11 hours a day, 6 or 7 days a week. As they do not have the same hukou status as locals, many employers do not provide them with the same benefits as local workers. Consequently, they are subject to institutional discrimination, including low wages and harsh working and living conditions, often contending with bosses who do not pay them or who expose them to dangerous equipment and toxic materials.

With goals of saving up enough to return home after a few years, migrant workers often put up with harsh working conditions and workplace abuses as long as they are earning more than they would at home. For example, toxins and health hazards are found in practically every industry including toys, furniture, clothing, shoes and electronic goods, with workers lacking in health protections such as protective masks and proper ventilation systems. Old or broken equipment without safety guards have resulted in millions of limb amputations in the last two decades.

The government has introduced **corporate social responsibility (CSR)** and worker safety monitoring programs to improve conditions. Although this has helped somewhat in reducing worker injuries, the fact remains that abuses still occur, from Chinese workers being exposed for years to toxic cadmium batteries while making toys for companies like Mattel and Toys R Us, to alleged instances of child labour being used at factories that supply goods for Wal-Mart.

Refugees

The China–Myanmar border is an area of much refugee movement. It is common for Chinese citizens to move to towns on the Burmese side to trade, while members of Myanmar's ethnic minorities cross into China unofficially as part of their daily lives, some just to buy cheaper vegetables.

China is also seeking to stem **illegal migration** by North Koreans fleeing oppression, by building a fence along portions of the border and imprisoning North Koreans deported by China.

Working age population

The National Bureau of Statistics says that China's working age population (ages 15–59) had declined in 2012 by 3.45 million, or 0.6%. Also, senior Communist Party officials estimate that China's total population will start declining after 2020, when the working age population will decrease by another 29 million.

This trend indicates an end of the **demographic dividend**, which is currently providing a large labour force and a low dependency ratio. China has already begun to see the consequences of this. A number of provinces, especially those on the coast, have experienced labour shortages, and have even called for the abolition of the one-child policy to help (see page 80). A smaller labour force could result in manufacturing jobs moving abroad and a higher dependency ratio, increasing health care and other social service costs.

The decline of the working age population and the end of the demographic dividend are largely due to the one-child policy, which is responsible for around 100 to 400 million fewer births per year. The one-child policy has also led to a dramatic gender discrepancy: compared to the global average of 103 boys for every 100 girls, China has 118 boys for every 100 girls.

Unemployment

A problem in China today is the growing rate of unemployment. In 2009, of the 130 million migrant workers who moved to the cities in search of employment, just over 20 million had to return home because they could not find work. This is around four times the population of Scotland. When added to the already large number of rural unemployed, some economists put the total number of rural unemployed at up to 40 million, twice the population of Australia. However, unemployment is not restricted to rural areas. In the same year, urban unemployment stood at 9 million people. In 2012 the estimated work force of China was around 1 billion people.

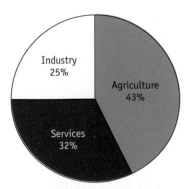

Figure 4.9 Employment by sector

Government responses

The Chinese Government says its working standards are consistent with international requirements and that products from child labour are not exported to the USA. It also points out the apparent hypocrisy of Western consumers being more than happy to buy low-cost Chinese products while they blame China for taking away jobs.

Enforcement of labour laws and standards is the duty of provincial governments, which often have a financial stake or interest in the businesses and in economic growth so there is little incentive to enforce laws. Health standards monitoring is also inadequate, with one inspector for every 35,000 workers.

In 2008, in response to widespread labour abuses of migrant workers, the government passed a new **Labour Contract Law**. This is seen as shifting the balance of power to the worker, but it is also perceived to be weak and often not enforced.

 Show your understanding

1 **(a)** Describe what is meant by the term 'migrant worker'.
   (b) Explain what working conditions and wages are like for migrant workers.
2 Explain one consequence of an end of the demographic dividend.
3 Describe the Chinese Government's response to employment and unemployment issues in China.

Develop your skills

4 'It is unlikely that with a decline in urban growth Chinese cities will increase in size, although it is true that the number employed in agriculture is still over 50%.' (*Ze Dhongi*)

   Using Figures 4.7 and 4.9, explain why Ze Dhongi could be accused of exaggeration.

Wealth and poverty

The **economic disparity** between urban and rural China is among the largest in the world. In recent decades many impoverished rural dwellers have flocked to the country's eastern cities, which have enjoyed a construction boom. By the beginning of 2012, city dwellers appeared to outnumber the rural population for the first time, according to official figures.

Today in China there are about 150 million people (15%) living below the United Nations poverty line of $1 a day and nearly 500 million people living on less than $2 a day. Some 85% of China's poor live in rural areas, with about 66% in western regions. China's poverty among ethnic minorities is three times higher than among Han Chinese and higher among children than adults (with 16% of boys and 17% of girls living in poverty).

Increasing income inequality

A Credit Suisse survey in 2010 found that, since 2004, the income for the top 10% of households had risen by 255% compared with 50% for the bottom 20% of households. Such growing inequality has led to an environment of mistrust and resentment. Although many Chinese may endorse and aspire to the lifestyles of the rich and famous, they still tend to resent the way the economic elite got their wealth. There is strong public opinion that corruption is the main reason for wealth inequalities.

Although economic growth has created vast wealth for some, it has widened inequalities between rich and poor with a rapid emergence of private wealth. The privatisation of state enterprises and the housing and social benefits that accompanied them, the compulsory purchase of rural land for industry and a construction boom have all allowed some citizens to accumulate enormous personal wealth that has not been evenly distributed.

Consumption

It is widely held that when a country reaches a certain level of development, its economic growth becomes increasingly driven by domestic consumption rather than investment and exports. China's astounding economic growth of the last three decades has been achieved primarily through industrial production, infrastructure-building, foreign investment and especially through exports. China's consumption rate (approximately 25% of GDP) is the lowest of any major economy. However, the Chinese have been consuming more in the last 30 years. For example, from 2007 to 2009, retail sales in China grew by 25% annually.

Experts predict that China's share of global consumption is expected to increase from 5.2% ($1.72 trillion) in 2009 to 23.1% ($15.94 trillion) in 2020, surpassing the USA as the largest consumer market in the world. Some believe that Chinese consumers are poised to transform the world.

Chinese middle class

A large and strong **middle class** that consumes is key to economic growth. There is no universal definition of middle class, but one common measure is income, with the bottom 20% of wage earners being lower class, the top 20% upper class and the remaining 60% middle class. Other factors can be education, occupation and lifestyle.

In 2005 China's National Bureau of Statistics stated that the urban middle class should have a yearly income of between 60,000 yuan ($7,255 in 2005 dollars) and 500,000 yuan ($60,459).

A 2010 Credit Suisse survey of Chinese households found that, between 2004 and 2009, the average household income of the 40%–60% income group grew by 98%.

Consumption of luxury goods

China is the world's largest consumer of luxury goods; in second place is Japan and then the USA. Most Chinese consumers of luxury goods are young and middle aged, whereas American consumers are middle aged and elderly. The average age of a Chinese Ferrari owner is 32 whereas in the USA it is 47. Similarly, the average age of a BMW owner in China is 30 versus 49 in the EU.

Figure 4.10 China is the world's largest consumer of luxury goods

Although economic reforms have lifted millions out of poverty and created a Consuming Class, they have also created a 'surviving' underclass.

Government responses

The government has introduced a **National Minimum Wage** and promised to increase it at a rate of 13% a year during the course of the five-year plan that runs until 2015. The minimum wages in 2011 ranged from 1,500 yuan (£152.79) per month in Shenzhen (the highest), to 870 yuan in Chongqing (the lowest). Nevertheless, in China the gap between rich and poor has widened into a chasm. About 13% of China's 1.33 billion people still live on less than $1.25 (79p) per day according to the United Nations Development Programme and average urban disposable income is just 21,810 yuan a year. Meanwhile, China has 2,700,000 millionaires and 251 billionaires.

Urban–rural divide

Inequality in China has now surpassed that in the USA, with a growing disparity between urban and rural areas. In 2010 rural residents had an annual average disposable income of 5,900 yuan ($898). That is less than one-third of the average disposable income of urban residents, which stood at 19,100 yuan ($2,900). This gap between urban disposable and rural income has persistently widened since 1978. Inequalities in income are reflected in household consumption patterns and the access those households have to basic consumer goods (Table 4.1).

Government responses

The government wants to help rural residents out of poverty. It has worked to raise minimum wages for migrant workers and improved rural incomes through **tax cuts**. It has also enforced labour contract laws. The government also tries to encourage labour-intensive industries to move to rural areas.

	Urban households			Rural households		
	1990	2000	2009	1990	2000	2009
Colour television	59	116.6	135.6	4.7	48.7	108.9
Cars	–	0.5	10.9	–	0.1	0.7
Motorcycles	1.9	18.8	22.4	0.9	21.9	56.6
Computers	–	9.7	65.7	–	0.5	7.5
Washing machines	78.4	90.5	96.0	9.1	28.6	53.1
Refrigerators	42.3	80.1	95.3	1.2	12.3	37.1
Air conditioners	0.34	30.8	106.8	–	1.3	12.2

Table 4.1 Ownership of household goods per 100 households, 1990–2009

Source: National Bureau of Statistics of China

Show your understanding

1 In your own words, explain what is meant by China's middle class.
2 Describe the economic disparity between urban and rural China.
3 Describe how the Chinese Government has responded to wealth inequalities.

Develop your skills

4 Using Table 4.1, what conclusions can you draw about urban and rural households in China? You should reach conclusions about the following:
   (a) The growth in rural ownership of colour television, washing machines and refrigerators.
   (b) The availability of consumer items in urban and rural areas in 2009.

Health care

After years of free market reform, China now has a **hybrid health care system** made up of an employer-based insurance scheme and state social service supplements. The private sector is now involved and has introduced a pay-as-you-go system. However, for many people, paying as they go is simply proving too expensive and they cannot afford to pay anything towards their health care. This means that, for millions of the country's less wealthy, prices have become a barrier with basic health care simply unaffordable.

However, China's Ministry of Health has set itself a target to introduce a universal health care system where people pay for only 20% of treatment by 2020. While they wait, some people are seeking out and attending the increasing number of cheap, illegal clinics – known as **black clinics** – which are operating particularly in rural areas.

It could be argued that China's health care system is turning into a **two-tier system**: one for the rich and one for the poor; one government-backed and regulated but expensive, the other illegal, unregulated and dangerous but cheap. Health is now subject to market forces: those with money can afford the best of care and those without money either go without treatment or seek help in black clinics. A recent World Bank report highlighted that 1 in 5 of China's poor blamed their poverty on having to pay health care bills.

Changing health needs

Chinese people are adopting more of a Western lifestyle, with its associated health problems (see 'Obesity' on page 73). The big killers are now cancer, heart disease and strokes, with 80% of people in China dying from one of these three conditions. The wealthier own cars and therefore cycle less. They can also afford richer diets and so eat less healthily, with more fatty foods and meat. They also smoke and drink more.

The problem for many poor Chinese is that these illnesses are expensive to treat and take many years of treatment. Paying for medical treatment can effectively bankrupt whole families. Government social insurance schemes can help with payments. Many millions of rural dwellers are joining rural health schemes whereby a small annual payment is matched by a payment from the state. This does

Case study: The Lee family

The Lee family knows all too well the levels of corruption and ever-increasing medical bills in China. Their mother is in a Beijing hospital suffering from cancer. They recently paid out £20,000 on an operation for her after being told initially it would cost £15,000. They are not poor, but feel that the hospital increased the price of the operation when they found out how wealthy they are.

'When my friend was visiting the hospital, the doctors asked him outright how wealthy we were and what type of car I drove. The very next day the cost of my mother's operation had gone up by £5,000. We have also given backhanders to doctors; this is common in our country. Before the operation I was told by a doctor that I should give money to those carrying it out. I gave £1,000 each to the surgeon and anaesthetist.'

provide some cover, but sometimes it is not enough. The state payments usually only cover a small part of the total medical bill, so contracting a chronic illness can still lead to bankruptcy.

Healthy China 2020

China's Ministry of Health is working towards providing basic health care for all its citizens. The **Healthy China 2020** programme will provide a universal national health service and promote equal access to public services in an attempt to copy the NHS in the UK.

At present, health care provision for the tens of millions of rural dwellers is inadequate and the cost of medical care to the urban poor is leading to severe inequality. It is hoped that this new programme will satisfy people's increased expectations, increase life expectancy and reduce the links between wealth and health inequalities, not only between rich and poor but also between rural and urban populations.

Obesity

Chinese people have recently begun to see increases in levels of obesity, although it is mostly confined to urban areas. Around one-third of city residents are overweight through what is known as the 'Western disease'. As Chinese people consume more and want more, they are subject to a more pressurised lifestyle where they take less exercise and have a less healthy diet, with a liking for fast food like McDonald's and Kentucky Fried Chicken.

Figure 4.11 China has seen increasing levels of obesity in recent years

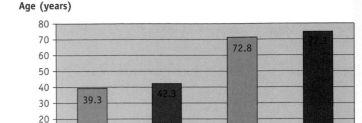

Age (years)

Figure 4.12 Life expectancy in China

FACT FILE

Smoking in China

- Almost 25% of the Chinese smoke.
- One out of every three cigarettes consumed worldwide is smoked in China.
- About 67% of men and 4% of women smoke.
- Among youths, about one-third of male teens smoke and nearly 8% of females.
- About 3,000 people die *every day* in China due to smoking.

Infant mortality rates

According to the United Nations Children's Fund (UNICEF), infant mortality tops the list of preventable causes of child death in China at 60%. In rural areas almost twice as many mothers die in childbirth as in urban areas. Also, infant and child mortality is almost three times higher in western than in eastern regions, and 2.5 times higher in rural than in urban areas.

Education

The education system in China is run by the state. All children are entitled to nine years of free education, usually between the ages of 6 and 15 (6 years of primary school and 3 years of middle school). After middle school, parents have to pay if children choose to continue to attend high school.

They can also opt to go to vocational schools to learn the skills necessary to get jobs such as technicians.

Before 1949 the literacy rate in China was 20%. In 2013 the literacy rate was 93%, with that for males at 96% and females at 90%.

Rural and urban students

Although most families in cities can afford to pay education fees after the age of 15, in rural parts of China many students have to stop their education then because of the cost. According to the World Bank, three main groups of people are prevented from continuing their education beyond the age of 15 because of poverty: the rural poor, girls and migrants.

However, the government is allocating more money and resources to rural schools and poverty-hit areas while enhancing the salaries of rural teachers in an effort to address the inequality and reduce regional and rural–urban education gaps. Educational facilities in rural schools such as books, science equipment and school buildings are being improved, and top teachers are being encouraged to move to rural schools.

More time and effort is going in to ensure that children of rural migrant workers receive proper schooling in urban cities. Increases in migration from rural to urban coastal areas in China have seen more migrant families, including young school-age children, moving to the cities. The school enrolment system in some areas is based on the hukou – the place of household registration (see page 67). This results in migrant children without a hukou being denied access to local schools in the cities. A recent survey found that although 100% of children of local Beijing residents were enrolled in primary and secondary schools, only 40% of migrant children were.

Nevertheless, in recent years a number of schools have been established to meet the educational needs of migrant children in some areas. These are schools established by migrant communities themselves without financial support from the state and most are run illegally because they are unable to obtain official approval.

12-year plan

The Chinese Government has drawn up a **12-year education plan** to improve rural and vocational training. It will run until 2020, with the government increasing the funding for scholarships in urban areas while also increasing funding for the renovation of primary and secondary schools in rural areas and offering free rural vocational training. This is to ensure that migrant workers who have lost their jobs in the cities have access to practical skills training when they return home.

The state is also committed to developing schools for ethnic minorities by adopting bilingual teaching systems and giving preferential treatment to students of minority ethnic groups in enrolment in schools and universities.

Private education

There are a growing number of private schools in China for wealthy Chinese as well as dozens of international private schools. Most international schools will only accept Chinese who hold a foreign passport, but Chinese public schools are required by law to accept children of legal foreign residents. There are over 70 schools approved by China's Ministry of Education to provide foreign instruction. Unlike local children, foreigners must pay a yearly tuition fee.

Corruption

Corruption within China's state-run education system has been blamed for causing inequality. Education through junior high school is supposed to be free, but in reality this is often not the case. As a child grows up, parents lacking connections must pay repeatedly for better educational opportunities. These illegal fees are especially difficult for the millions of struggling migrant workers who have moved to urban areas.

Corruption is widespread in every part of Chinese society, and education is no exception. Nearly everything has a price, from school admissions to placement in top classes. Even front-row seats near the blackboard are up for sale.

I had to pay $4,800 into a bank account to enrol my daughter in junior school. At the bank, I was stunned to find that officials from the district education committee had a list of students and how much each family had to pay. I was also forced to sign a document saying the fee was a 'voluntary donation'. Of course, I knew it was illegal – but if I didn't pay, my daughter wouldn't have got in.

FACT FILE

Education

- Chinese children must attend school for nine years.
- Chinese youths between the ages of 15 and 24 have a 99% literacy rate.
- Private schools were not allowed until the 1980s.
- Local governments and businesses keep an eye on secondary education: high schools and upper middle schools are run by state and local governments as well as local business leaders.
- After-school education is an important aspect of the Chinese education system and it is watched over by the Communist Youth League.

Housing

China's population has grown by about one-third in 30 years, from 1 billion in 1982, to about 1.33 billion in 2013. This has triggered a massive challenge in providing affordable homes. China has chosen to make home ownership for all a priority, as well as the basis of its social protection and welfare system.

The government has therefore decided that the way to overcome increasing housing shortages, especially in crowded cities, is to have private developers build large apartment blocks and allow people to buy them. Instead of paying welfare benefits, it now gives support towards buying property.

Private developers

Private developers are now building more private apartments. Home ownership is growing fast, especially in larger and more modern cities like Shanghai, where over 50% of houses are now owner-occupied. However, this prosperity is not universal: in some provinces, less than 10% of the population are home owners. The main reason for this is that some simply cannot afford it. House prices are constantly rising, making it very difficult for many people to get on to the property ladder.

Affordable housing

It is estimated that an apartment in China's urban areas costs around eight times the average annual income of a household. In rural China, this jumps to 29 times. This means that home ownership is beyond the means of around 60% of China's urban households and 85% of rural migrants who are flocking into the cities every year. This has led to young people from the middle classes being known as belonging to a 'sandwich class'. This means that they do not have enough money to buy a property, while at the same time there are not enough properties available for them to rent.

Compulsory eviction

Every piece of land in China remains under the control of the state, and local officials can take over land and evict residents by confiscating homes to make way for urban development. These compulsory or forced evictions are a major worry for Chinese residents and have recently led to people rioting against having their homes seized. Bullying tactics have been used by local officials to force people out of their homes, including the use of violence and cutting off water and power supplies.

Many thousands of people in China have been forcibly evicted, or 'relocated' as the government likes to call it, to make way for major projects including getting Beijing ready to host the 2008 Olympics. For example, according to Amnesty International former lawyer Ni Yulan was tried on charges of 'picking quarrels' and 'fraud'; she was forcibly evicted from her home in 2008, before the Beijing Olympics; and she was paralysed from the waist down as a result of beatings in detention.

WON'T SELL UP? ENJOY LIVING IN THE MIDDLE OF A MOTORWAY!

Duck farmer Luo Baogen and his wife lived in an apartment in the city of Wenling, in Zhejiang province, China. The elderly couple refused to vacate their home when the authorities announced the construction of a new road, as they believed that the compensation offered for relocation was not enough.

Nevertheless, the building work went ahead, and cars were forced to drive around the building, situated in the middle of the road. To ensure the couple's safety, adjacent rooms in the building were left intact but all their neighbours had moved out.

After a year, the couple accepted increased compensation in December 2012, and their house was demolished at last.

Adapted from news sources

Figure 4.13 Luo Baogen's home in Wenling city is demolished

Property owners in China who refuse to move to make way for development are known as 'Nail Householders', referring to a stubborn nail that is not easy to remove from a piece of old wood and cannot be pulled out with a hammer. However, since 2010 the government has ensured that anyone relocated is given at least the property's market value by way of compensation.

Social discontent manifests itself in protests by farmers and workers. Tens of thousands of people travel to Beijing each year to lodge petitions with the authorities in the hope of finding redress for alleged corruption, land seizures and evictions.

Government responses

The Communist Party is expanding the construction of low-income housing to reduce inequality of access to affordable housing as house prices rocket upwards, effectively shutting out an increasing number of Chinese from buying homes. China plans to build 36 million housing units under the five-year plan (2011–15), including 10 million units at a cost of around $200 billion.

However, according to the China Development Research Foundation, local governments have shirked their responsibility of building affordable houses for those on a low-income. Instead, they diverted the money elsewhere. For example, recent audits conducted by the central government found that close to 3 billion yuan ($490 million) allocated for low-income housing developments had been spent on other projects.

Show your understanding

1 Why might China's health care system be described as a two-tier system, one for the rich and one for the poor?
2 Describe the Healthy China 2020 programme.
3 Describe the inequalities in access to education between rural and urban students.
4 Explain what the 12-year education plan is.
5 Explain why corruption is a problem in education in China.
6 (a) Explain the problems of housing in China today.
   (b) Describe what the Chinese Government is doing about housing problems in China.

Branch out

7 Working in pairs, create a Fact File indicating the health, education and housing issues facing the Chinese people.

Law, order and human rights

What you will learn:

1 The extent of crime in China and how the Chinese Government is responding to it.

2 About human rights issues in China and how they are viewed by the world.

The extent of crime in China today

China has a low crime rate. Private gun ownership is banned and violent crime is relatively rare. The Chinese are generally very honest and they rarely steal. Tourists sometimes tell stories of leaving behind unwanted clothes in their hotel room only to have an employee at the hotel show up at the airport or train station to return their clothes.

Although China is still a relatively safe place, violent crime is on the rise. A report by the Academy of Social Sciences noted a 'dramatic increase' in violent crime. Criminals from different regions have different specialties. North-east China is famous for armed robbers. Xinjiang is said to be home to the best pickpockets. Wenzhou in Zhejiang produces car thieves. Many people smugglers are based in Fujian.

The relatively well-off town of Aodi in Zhejiang built a 'Great Wall' around the town to keep thieves out. The wall is 7 m high and nearly 1 m thick and is built in the style of the famous Great Wall of China with the exception of a swipe card system that is used to get through the double-doored gate. The 270 villagers were concerned about rising number of thefts of mobile phones, computers and cash, and raised the $75,000 themselves needed to build the wall.

SHOPLIFTING GANG OF PREGNANT WOMEN CAUGHT AFTER MORE THAN A DECADE

A month-long police operation has finally cracked the Big Belly Gang, a band of pregnant thieves that ransacked shopping centres in Hangzhou and was responsible for the majority of in-store thefts in the province. The maternal crime ring, whose members met each day outside the local school gates, was dubbed the 'Big Belly Gang'. The police captured all 47 gang members, of whom 22 were pregnant at the time. The gang exploited China's leniency towards expectant and new mothers.

Adapted from news sources

Cyber crime

According to *Global Times*, in 2012 losses from Internet crimes in China totalled an estimated $46.4 billion. Fraud, prostitution, pyramid selling and personal information theft were the most common crimes committed and 700,000 users fall prey to Internet crime in China every day.

In 2012 state media reported that Chinese security officials had arrested 10,000 suspects and broken up 600 criminal gangs during a crackdown on online and bank card crime during which online shoppers had been defrauded out of almost $5 million between 2011 and 2012. In 2013 the police intensified the crackdown and formed partnerships with financial institutions to bring about a long-term mechanism on fighting crimes in the financial sector. As a result, 900 million yuan ($147 million) of stolen money has been recovered.

Migrant workers and peasants

Many of those arrested for petty thefts are migrant workers. They are blamed for many crimes and are held responsible for the rising crime rate. People also blame the general 'get-rich-quick' mentality.

There is also a rising crime rate in rural areas. There have been cases where innocent people have been killed in their homes during pitched battles between rival villages while the police stood by and did nothing. One such battle was triggered by a schoolboy fight that escalated to pitched battles in which villagers built ramparts and fired cannon made from empty gas cylinders.

Juvenile crime

Juvenile crime is a growing problem in China. Youths are now believed to account for around 10% of all crimes. Cases include one in which a 16-year-old Beijing high school student killed his mother for 'being too strict', taking £30 from her pocket and heading to an Internet café. In another case a 15-year-old Beijing student stabbed a friend 17 times with a fruit knife for flirting with her boyfriend. In Guanxi, a 23-year-old student was executed after killing four roommates with a hammer over a card game. Another youth was caught pouring battery acid on zoo animals.

The increase is blamed on broken homes, a lack of parental control and too much pressure on young people to excel. One study found that 60% of juvenile criminals were drop outs and 60% had truancy records. The Communist Party blames the problem on 'spiritual pollution' from foreign movies and television programmes.

Efforts to reduce juvenile crime have seen laws passed that punish the parents of the young criminals. In recent years, help and education programmes have been set up involving juvenile delinquents, their parents, other relatives and people in their community.

Abductions and human trafficking

There are many unexplained disappearances in China. Newspapers and bulletin boards are filled with notices of missing persons. Some no doubt have fled to seek a better life somewhere else, but many are believed to be victims of foul play. Some are young girls thought to have been abducted and sold as wives.

Human rights

The UK Government's views

The UK Government says that there has been significant progress on social and economic rights in China over the past 25 years: ordinary people can now usually travel freely, choose who to marry and where to work. However, problems still remain, particularly on civil and political rights.

Despite signing the **International Covenant on Civil and Political Rights (ICCPR)** in 1998, China has still not ratified it. China is making progress, but there remain a number of areas where it currently fails to meet ICCPR standards.

The system of re-education through labour and other forms of 'administrative detention' remains in place, although its scope and the maximum length of sentences are being reduced. Torture is still a widespread problem. Senior leaders now appear to recognise it as such and are beginning to introduce measures that act to prevent torture, such as the tape recording of police interrogations.

The freedoms of expression, religion and association are severely restricted. However, on 1 January 2007 China introduced new regulations for foreign correspondents, who no longer have to seek case-by-case permission to conduct interviews.

The use of the death penalty remains unacceptably high, although the Supreme People's Court now reviews all death sentences and there is some reason to believe that this has led to a reduction in its use. Tibet and Xinjiang are still subject to particularly repressive security regimes.

The UK Government takes a multi-layered approach to engaging China on human rights. It raises a broad range of human rights issues, together with certain individual cases, through regular UK–China Human Rights Dialogue. The 20th round of the Dialogue took place in Nanjing in January 2012.

The British Government does not support Tibetan independence; it regards Tibet as part of the People's Republic of China. It regularly urges the Chinese Government to engage in serious negotiations with the Dalai Lama's representatives, as it sees this as the only lasting way to build a peaceful, sustainable and legitimate solution for Tibet.

ICT task

Compile a Fact File on the views of the UK Government about China's human rights record. Go to the UK Foreign and Commonwealth Office's website to help you: www.gov.uk/government/organisations/foreign-commonwealth-office

Amnesty International's views

Amnesty International is very critical of the lack of human rights and limited democracy in China.

- Muslims, Buddhists and Christians, who practised their religion outside officially sanctioned channels, and Falun Gong practitioners, were tortured, harassed, arbitrarily detained, imprisoned and faced other serious restrictions on their right to freedom of religion.

- The authorities continued to pursue a systematic, nationwide, often violent campaign against the Falun Gong, a spiritual group banned since 1999 as a 'heretical cult'. Practitioners who refused to renounce their faith were at risk of escalating levels of torture and other ill-treatment. The authorities operated illegal detention centres, informally referred to as 'brainwashing centres', for this process.

- Police deprived hundreds of thousands of people of their liberty by placing them in administrative detention, without recourse to independent courts. The authorities operated hundreds of places of detention, including 'black jails' and Legal Education Training Centres where they held thousands arbitrarily, and where torture, sometimes leading to death, was an established method of 'correction' or deterrence.

- At the end of 2011 and beginning of 2012, several human rights defenders who consistently called for political reform were sentenced to long jail terms. Sentences included ten years for Guizhou human rights forum leader Chen Xi and activist Li Tie, nine years for Sichuan human rights activist Chen Wei, seven years for Zhejiang Democratic Party member Zhu Yufu and, at the end of 2012, eight years for Jiangsu internet activist Cao Haibo, who set up an online group to discuss constitutional law and democracy.

- The authorities continued to repress Tibetans' right to enjoy and promote their own culture as well as their rights to freedom of religion, expression, peaceful association and assembly. Socioeconomic discrimination against ethnic Tibetans persisted unchecked. During the year, at least 83 ethnic Tibetan monks, nuns and lay people set themselves on fire, bringing the total number of **self-immolations** in Tibetan populated areas in China to at least 95 since February 2009.

- The authorities maintained their 'strike hard' campaign, criminalising what they labelled 'illegal religious' and 'separatist' activities, and clamping down on peaceful expressions of cultural identity. In May, nine Uighurs were sentenced to prison terms ranging from six to 15 years for participating in alleged 'illegal religious activities'. In June, an 11-year-old boy, Mirzahid, died in custody after being detained for studying in an 'illegal religious school'.

Based on Amnesty International Annual Reports, 2012 and 2013

The one-child policy

China's one-child policy has been in place for more than three decades. It restricts couples in urban areas to having only one child. There has been growing resentment across China against the enforcement of strict family planning rules. Some of the regulations have been relaxed, allowing second children to those in rural areas or to parents who are themselves both only children. However, violators still face fines and problems registering their children for school and medical care. There have also been reports of more brutal methods, including forced abortions and sterilisations conducted by overzealous local officials. There was shock in June 2012 when photos were leaked of a woman lying next to the foetus she had been forced to abort under the one-child policy.

Figure 4.14 China's one-child policy has been in place for more than three decades

In 2013 police in China detained two government workers after a baby was killed in a dispute over a violation of the country's one-child policy. The 13-month-old boy was dropped as family planning officials tried to fine his parents £4,000 for having three children. The infant was then run over by the officials' van.

The Internet and the media

The Internet

Through its Golden Shield Project, or the 'Great Firewall' as it is known, the Chinese Government monitors all Internet communication. It blocks access to forbidden sites like the BBC and the New York Times. Also blocked are websites such as Wikipedia, Facebook and Twitter, and human rights sites such as Amnesty International. Thousands of **cyber police** watch the web, while Internet cafés are closely monitored. Filtering targets material deemed politically and socially sensitive.

In 2009, after serious unrest in Xinjiang, the Chinese Government closed the region's Internet from both the rest of China and the world for a period of ten months. In 2011 **Reporters Without Borders** listed China as an 'enemy of the Internet' and 68 Internet users were imprisoned in January 2012.

WWW

For further information on the non-profit organisation Reporters Without Borders, go to www.rsf.org

Not only has Chinese authoritarian rule survived the Internet, but the state has used this technology to enable it to exercise better control of its own society. China's party-state has deployed an army of cyber police, hardware engineers, software developers, web monitors and paid online propagandists to watch, filter, censor and guide Chinese Internet users.

The goal is not to make it impossible but rather to make it as inconvenient as possible to access information or take any real steps that may undermine the government's and the party's authority and legitimacy. With 564 million Internet users at the end of 2012 (China Internet Network Information Centre), China has the world's largest net-using population. Mobile platforms are the main means of access and social networking has seen phenomenal growth, with the numbers of microblog users reaching 309 million in 2012.

Newspapers

There are more than 2,000 newspapers to choose from in China. Each city has its own, which is usually published by the local government, as well as a local Communist Party daily. Newspaper content is tightly controlled by the government. The publications must stay within the guidelines of what is allowed through a combination of government directives and self-censorship.

Television

Television is a popular news source in China, with around 1.2 billion viewers. All broadcast media are owned by, or affiliated with, the CPC or a government agency: there are no privately owned television or radio stations. State-run Chinese Central TV, provincial and municipal stations offer more than 2,000 channels, but the **Central Propaganda Department** lists subjects that are off-limits to domestic broadcast media with the government maintaining the authority to approve all programming. Foreign-made television programmes must be approved prior to broadcast.

China spends a lot of money on television, radio, online and press outlets targeted at international audiences, aiming to extend its political influence and boost its image abroad.

 Show your understanding

1 Describe the extent of cyber crime in China today.
2 Explain the main reasons for juvenile crime in China.
3 What actions has the Chinese Government taken against religious and minority nationality groups in China?
4 Describe the restrictions on Internet use in China.

Chapter 5

Development issues in Africa

A divided and unequal world?

Developed and developing countries

We are lucky enough to live in a **developed** country with a high standard of living, good health services, high literacy levels and low infant mortality rates. Scotland is a wealthy nation with an economy based on industry, trade and new technologies. In Scotland we also enjoy rights, a safe and stable society and a democratic political system. Some other countries around the world that are considered developed nations include the USA, Germany, France, Japan and Italy. Most developed nations are in the northern hemisphere.

What you will learn:

1 The differences between developed and developing countries.

2 The background and needs of Africa.

By contrast, many countries in the southern hemisphere are considered to be **developing** nations. In these countries living standards are low, illiteracy and infant mortality rates are high and health care services are poor. The economy of a developing nation is generally based on agriculture and there is a lack of modern technology and labour skills. Furthermore, society lacks infrastructure and the political system may be

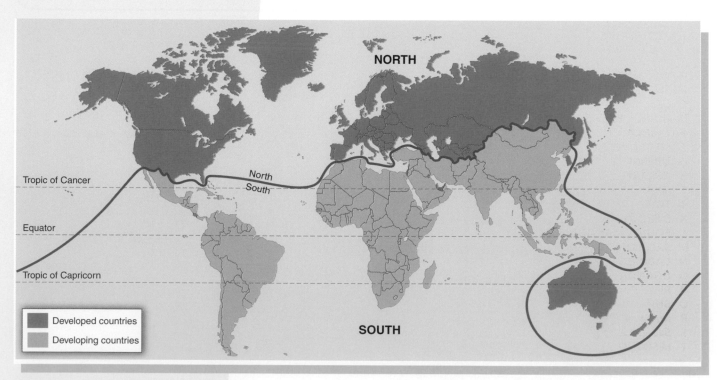

Figure 5.1 A clear North–South divide

undemocratic and corrupt. The developing world is also sometimes referred to as the **third world** and it relies heavily on the developed world for aid and assistance.

The world's poorest continent

Africa is the second-largest continent on Earth. Not surprisingly for such a huge land mass, it is home to an incredible variety of climates, cultures, animals and plants. Africa is home to the largest desert on Earth, the Sahara, and the longest river, the Nile. The continent is made up of 54 independent countries that together contain over 1 billion people. The population of Africa has grown quickly from 220 million in 1950 to just over 1 billion by 2013. In many African countries, particularly those south of the Sahara, more than 40% of the population are below 15 years of age.

Africa is endowed with a rich bounty of **natural resources** such as oil, diamonds, gold, iron,

A WESTERN SAHARA
B SENEGAL
C GAMBIA
D GUINEA BISSAU
E GUINEA
F SIERRA LEONE
G LIBERIA
H CÔTE D'IVOIRE
I GHANA
J TOGO
K DJIBOUTI
L EQUATORIAL GUINEA
M SAO TOME & PRINCIPE
N CABINDA
O UGANDA
P RWANDA
Q BURUNDI
R MALAWI
S SWAZILAND
T LESOTHO

Figure 5.2 Africa

copper, timber and tropical fruits. However, of the 20 poorest countries in the world, 18 are in Africa – including the poorest, Democratic Republic (DR) of Congo – and around 50% of sub-Saharan Africa's population lives on less than £1 a day. How can this be the case with such natural riches? You can see from Table 5.1 the stark differences in wealth, health and education between Democratic Republic of Congo, a developing nation, and the UK, an industrialised developed country.

ICT task

Working in pairs, use the Internet to choose an African country (excluding DR Congo). Create a Fact File of the country detailing information on population statistics, health, education and the economy.

	DR Congo	UK
Population	74 million	63 million
Health:		
Life expectancy	42 years	79 years
People with HIV/AIDS	4.2%	0.2%
Immunisation levels:		
TB	68%	100%
Polio	55%	91%
Measles	54%	81%
Education:		
Male literacy	73%	100%
Female literacy	50%	100%
Primary school enrolment	50%	99%
Secondary school enrolment	19%	98%
GDP per capita	$300	$36,500
Women and children:		
Risk of death in childbirth	540 in 100,000	12 in 100,000
Infant mortality rate	77 in 1000	5 in 1000

Table 5.1 Comparing DR Congo and the UK

Show your understanding

1 **(a)** What are the main features of a developed country? Name five such countries.
   (b) What are the main features of a developing country? Name five such countries.
2 How many countries are there in Africa and what is its total population?
3 What percentage of sub-Saharan Africa's population live on less than £1 a day?
4 Look at Table 5.1, the comparison between DR Congo and the UK. Describe the differences between:
   (a) immunisation levels
   (b) literacy rates
   (c) infant mortality rates.

Develop your skills

5 'Africa has a shortage of natural resources.' (*Anne Docherty*)

   Explain why Anne Docherty could be accused of exaggeration.

Causes and consequences of a lack of development

What you will learn:

1 The social, economic and political reasons why some African countries are underdeveloped.
2 The consequences of underdevelopment on Africa and its population.

A complex variety of factors have combined to prevent Africa from developing as it should. Some of these factors are the fault of African countries themselves and others are caused by developed rich nations who have exploited and continue to **exploit** Africa's plentiful resources. The lack of development in Africa has resulted in many serious problems for the people of Africa, such as extreme poverty, disease and war. This lack of development is an international issue of huge importance and one that needs to be addressed by the world immediately.

Social factors

Health

HIV/AIDS

In 2012 in sub-Saharan Africa an estimated 1.2 million people died of HIV/AIDS and a further 1.8 million people were newly infected, adding to the estimated total of 24 million already living with HIV. A report published by the United Nations warns that HIV/AIDS will kill half of all 15-year-olds in Botswana and Zimbabwe by 2015 if something is not done. Clearly there is an HIV/AIDS epidemic in Africa that shows no signs of slowing down. In killing 6,000 people a day, HIV/AIDS claims more lives than war, famine and floods combined.

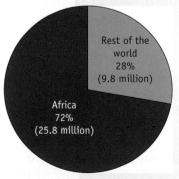

Figure 5.3 Africa has 11 million AIDS orphans

Figure 5.4 The global HIV/AIDS epidemic

HIV/AIDS in Africa

- Approximately 72% of all people in the world who are infected by HIV/AIDS live in Africa.
- Half of all people become infected by the age of 25.
- Access to anti-retroviral drugs is impossible for many Africans.
- HIV/AIDS is a major cause of children being orphaned.
- HIV/AIDS hinders social and economic development.
- The problem has been exacerbated by poverty, illiteracy, weak educational and public health systems, and the low social status of women.

The effects of the HIV/AIDS epidemic on social development are massive. Medical services cannot cope with the problem and hospitals are overrun with HIV/AIDS sufferers alone. In Botswana around one-third of people are suffering from the disease. This severely lowers life expectancy and prevents people who are suffering from working and contributing to the economy.

Malaria

Malaria is one of the leading causes of death and disease in the developing world. It is a preventable and treatable infectious disease transmitted by mosquitoes. The symptoms include fever, chills, muscle ache and hallucinations. These can lead on to more serious symptoms such as kidney failure and brain disease. If left untreated, malaria will kill. It is responsible for the deaths of more than 1 million people each year, most of them in sub-Saharan Africa, with 75% of those deaths occurring in children under five. It is estimated that a child dies every 45 seconds from the disease.

The affects of malaria on a country are similar to HIV/AIDS. As malaria affects so many young people, it hinders their education and therefore the future workforce of a country.

Famine and malnutrition

Famine is brought about by the shortage or inability of people to obtain food. This might be caused by low food production resulting from **drought** or other factors such as **armed conflict** or **bad governance**. Around one-third of all people who live in sub-Saharan Africa are undernourished, with an estimated 275 million people in Africa going hungry every day. Children are the most visible victims of malnutrition. Those who are poorly nourished suffer up to 160 days of illness each year. Poor nutrition plays a role in around half of all child deaths in Africa. Malnutrition magnifies the effect of every disease, including measles and malaria.

Education

Figure 5.5 Students in an Ethiopian classroom

The education a child experiences in Africa is very different to the experience of a child in Scotland. In African countries, enrolment is the lowest in the world with 33 million children not attending primary school. When pupils do attend, they are faced with a lack of basic facilities and resources as well as class sizes of anything between 40 and 70.

The amount of debt owed by African countries means that they cannot afford to spend the required amount of money needed or provide free education to their citizens. It is estimated that because of a lack of finance, secondary education can only be offered to 36% of children in sub-

Saharan Africa. Without an adequate education system, any country will fail to prosper. A skilled and educated workforce is required for a country to move towards development.

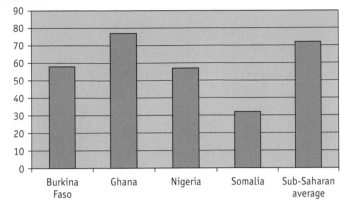

% enrolled

Figure 5.6 Primary school enrolment in selected African countries

Economic factors

Debt

Debt has long been seen as a major obstacle to development. Africa has a $300 billion debt bill, with countries on average spending a combined $14 billion annually repaying this debt. With African countries spending billions repaying their debts, they have less to spend on basic social infrastructure such as schools and hospitals.

The cycle of debt prevents many African countries developing at any considerable rate. Many African governments have borrowed money from the **International Monetary Fund (IMF)** or the **World Bank (WB)** to finance development. However, these institutions attach high interest rates to their loans, which results in massive repayments for many years. They also attach strict conditions when lending money, such as the requirement of African countries to spend a large amount of their revenue (20–40%) repaying the debt, which, in turn, cuts the amount of government spending on development.

Africa has also had its problems with **odious debt**. This is debt that has, mainly in decades past, been loaned to corrupt African governments by rich nations and been misspent or **embezzled**. The country and its people are then shackled with repaying the debt even although no money was ever spent to the benefit of its citizens.

 Added value

Research the affects of either AIDS/HIV or malaria on a specific African country. How has the disease hindered the development of that country? You could present your findings as a blog or Fact File.

To **embezzle** is to steal money that has been entrusted to you but belongs to someone else.

Show your understanding

1 **(a)** Outline some of the statistics that show there is an HIV/AIDS epidemic in Africa.
   (b) What are the effects of the HIV/AIDS epidemic on Africa?
2 What is malaria and what are its symptoms?
3 **(a)** In what ways is education in Africa different from that in Scotland?
   (b) Why is an adequate education system important for a country?

Develop your skills

4 Using Figure 5.6, reach a conclusion about education levels in Africa.

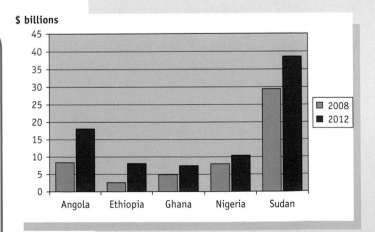

$ billions

Figure 5.7 Levels of debt in selected African countries ($ billions), 2008 and 2012

Source: *CIA World Factbook*

Case study: Angola and the burden of debt

Figure 5.8 Angola's flag

Angola is a nation rich in natural resources; it is Africa's second largest oil producer and also has a wealth of diamonds, iron ore and coffee. These natural resources should mean that the country is economically rich, yet this is not the case because of its troubled history of civil war and huge accumulation of foreign debts that have resulted from this. During the civil war that lasted from 1975 to 2002, the Angolan Government borrowed money from rich nations to fund its military. Angola's current debt therefore stands at $18.1 billion. This means that the country spends 6.8% of its GDP on loan repayments and only 1.5% on health.

In 2005 the world's richest countries agreed to cancel the debt of many of Africa's poorest countries. Countries that had excessive debt to the IMF or the WB had their debt cancelled, allowing them to divert funds into social development. For example, when Zambia's $4 billon debt was cancelled, the government introduced free health care for people living in rural areas, scrapping fees which for years had made health care inaccessible for millions. In Ghana, debt cancellation has been used with success to fund free early education and, in Mali, the funds were invested in improving the water supply and roads. However, the 2005 debt cancellation saw only around 60% of Africa's debt cancelled and many countries are still indebted to the IMF, the WB or the developed world.

Trade

Being rich in natural resources, Africa should be a prosperous continent with many products available to trade and sell to the rest of the world. If Africa could earn more through trade, countries would be able to rely less on foreign aid and loans. In 1980 Africa had a 6% share of world trade. By 2013 this had dropped to just 3%. If it could regain just an additional 1% share of global trade, it would earn $70 billion more in exports each year – several times more than what the region currently receives in foreign aid.

Trade varies greatly from country to country. Sudan and Nigeria are blessed with large **oil reserves** and can export millions of barrels per day. Countries like Malawi and Ethiopia depend heavily on growing and exporting **cash crops** like tea and coffee. Buyers from developed nations can force down the price of these cash crops and therefore reduce the finance flowing into developing countries. **Lack of infrastructure** is also a huge problem for many African nations and the transportation of goods is not always easy. This severely hinders trade between African countries.

Fairtrade

Figure 5.9 Fairtrade is about better prices and decent working conditions for farmers and workers in the developing world

Fairtrade is a worldwide movement that aims to create a fair trading system that ensures farmers in developing countries receive fair prices for their produce. It has grown in recent years, with many large companies signing up to the strategy. For example, all the coffee that Starbucks sells in the UK is made from coffee beans purchased according to Fairtrade standards.

Show your understanding

1   (a) What is Africa's current level of debt?
    (b) From which institutions do African countries borrow most of their money?
    (c) What conditions placed on debt causes problems for African countries?
    (d) What is 'odious debt'?
2   Read the case study on Angola.
    (a) Why should Angola be a rich nation?
    (b) Why is Angola in serious debt?
3   'When rich countries cancelled some of Africa's debt, many countries benefited.' Do you agree or disagree with this statement? Justify your answer.
4   Describe the problems Africa faces in trading with the global market.
5   What is the Fairtrade movement?

Develop your skills

6   Using Figure 5.7, reach a conclusion about the levels of debt in selected African countries.

Political factors

The effects of armed conflict

Armed conflict can tear a country apart and have devastating effects on social and economic development. Over the last few decades, many African nations have been locked in **civil war**. These countries include Sudan, Somalia, Mali, DR Congo, Angola and Rwanda, to name a few. In many cases civil war rages for decades and it can take a country years to recover and reconstruct after the conflict has ceased.

> A **civil war** is a war between groups, factions or inhabitants within the same country.

> **Genocide** is the deliberate killing of a large group of people, especially those of a particular ethnic group or nationality.

Case study: Armed conflict in Sudan

Figure 5.10 A rebel soldier in Sudan

The civil war in Sudan lasted from 1983 until 2005 and cost the lives of 1.5 million people. Continuing conflict in the western region of Darfur has driven 2 million people from their homes and killed more than 200,000. The United Nations has accused pro-government forces of carrying out a targeted **genocide** against the non-Arab population of Darfur. The burning of villages, mass murder, rape and child abduction have been commonplace in the last few years.

The infant death rate is very high in Sudan, with one in eight children not living to see their fifth birthday. The continuing conflict in Darfur is preventing many people from accessing safe drinking water and adequate sanitation facilities. Many of the 2 million who have fled their homes are now **refugees** in the neighbouring country of Chad.

Being rich in resources such as oil, cotton and gold, Sudan should be a leader in development in Africa, but because of decades of armed conflict the country is lacking basic infrastructure with over 40% of its citizens living below the poverty line.

Case study: Child soldiers

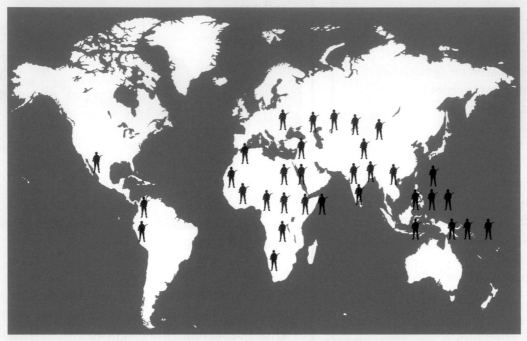

Figure 5.11 Countries with child soldiers fighting in conflict

As a direct result of armed conflict, many vulnerable children are caught up in war. It may seem unfair enough that a child's life is torn apart by war – perhaps through being orphaned – but in several countries in Africa children are actually being forced to take part in wars fighting as child soldiers. It is estimated that there are 250,000 child soldiers in the world, with 80% of those in Africa. Currently child soldiers are being used in armed conflicts in Central African Republic, Chad, DR Congo, Mali, Somalia and Sudan.

Why use children as soldiers?

Children are used as soldiers because they are easier to control, condition and brainwash. They do not eat much food, do not need to be paid and have an underdeveloped sense of danger, so they are easier to send into the line of fire. In many cases children are given drugs and develop addictions that mean they are more likely to follow orders to feed their dependency.

The psychological effects on children are felt long after the fighting finishes. Many child soldiers are desensitised to violence and have seen and done things that can leave lasting mental scars. If a child manages to escape war, they might not be able to return home because they have been cut off from their family. Some child soldiers are forced to kill a family member or neighbour just so they can never go back. Furthermore, most child soldiers will have missed out on school and, without an education, they have very poor future prospects.

Figure 5.12 As a direct result of armed conflict, many vulnerable children are caught up in war

EX-CHILD-SOLDIER: 'SHOOTING BECAME JUST LIKE DRINKING A GLASS OF WATER'

Figure 5.13 Ishmael Beah

When a teenager in Sierra Leone, Ishmael Beah's family were killed in the country's vicious civil war, which lasted from 1991 to 2002. Desperate for help, Ishmael says he wandered the countryside with a group of other children who had lost their families in similar circumstances. They stumbled upon a group of breakaway rebel soldiers who took them in, gave them food and shelter and then trained them to kill.

Ishmael says 'Somebody being shot in front of you, or you yourself shooting somebody, became just like drinking a glass of water. Children who refused to fight, kill or showed any weakness were dealt with ruthlessly. Emotions weren't allowed. For example, two 9-year-old boys cried because they missed their mother and they were shot', he says.

Ishmael fought with the group for 2 years before being rescued by UNICEF. He was then taken to a rehab centre in the capital, Freetown, where he spent 8 months learning about what happened to him and readjusting to life after the war. He now works for the UN as a goodwill ambassador and aims to help children who have suffered like him.

Adapted from news sources

www

Go to www.warchild.org.uk to further investigate the issue of child soldiers.

Bad governance and corruption

A major factor that has hindered development in Africa is the lack of fair and transparent governance. Bad governance means that a country will suffer as taxes are not collected and so cannot be spent on key services vital for public use such as schools and hospitals. Institutions such as the police, the military and the legal system may not operate in a just and impartial manner, compromising people's human rights.

Corruption has also been a huge problem in African politics. It has been stated that the day corruption ends in Africa is the very day we shall see the end of poverty, war, disease and famine. The lack of democracy has allowed many dictators to remain in power for decades, enjoying lavish lifestyles while the people starve. Money and aid that should flow to the population and be spent on health centres or primary schools is siphoned off into the bank accounts of government officials. Former Central African Republic dictator Jean-Bedel Bokassa was infamous for his corrupt ways in managing to amass a personal fortune of over $100 million while living in a palace surrounded by gold and diamonds, at the same time that the population of the country barely survived on $1 a day.

It is estimated that corruption costs the continent around $150 billion a year, with Somalia perceived to be the most corrupt nation on Earth in 2012.

Other factors affecting development

Climate change

Because of climate change, Africa is on average 0.5°C warmer than it was 100 years ago. However, temperatures have risen much higher in some areas such as a part of Kenya, which has become 3.5°C hotter in the past 20 years. Changes in the weather have meant that farmers find it more difficult to work the land and grow crops. This, in turn, is causing unemployment, loss of earnings and famine.

 Show your understanding

1 What is civil war and what impact can it have on a country?
2 Read the case study on armed conflict in Sudan. Describe the effects of the civil war on the people of Sudan.
3 Read the case study on child soldiers.
   (a) What is the estimated number of child soldiers in the world?
   (b) Why are children used as soldiers?
   (c) What are the effects of being a soldier on a child?
4 Read the story of a war child survivor and describe Ishmael's experiences.
5 What are the main features of bad governance?

Develop your skills

6 'Corruption is only a minor problem in African politics.' (*Paul Macdonald*)
   Explain why Paul Macdonald could be accused of exaggeration.

Natural disasters

Drought and floods are common in Africa and increasing because of climate change. Natural disasters can affect food and water supplies and have a major impact on people's lives. The financial cost of a natural disaster can exceed $1 billion and therefore place a great strain on government resources.

What efforts are being made to help and respond to Africa's needs?

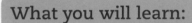

What you will learn:

1 How developed nations are working to help Africa.
2 The work of the African Union.
3 The work of the United Nations in Africa.
4 How NGOs are helping Africa.

You have studied the various problems and challenges that are blighting the continent of Africa and preventing African countries from sustained development. But what is being done to help, aid and support Africa? Individual countries, non-governmental organisations (NGOs) and international organisations are all working to improve the situation in Africa and address the many issues faced. Unfortunately, the vast array of challenges that Africa faces changes from one country to the next. Providing the appropriate support is often difficult and complicated.

How developed nations are assisting Africa

Aid is assistance that can help poorer countries overcome the challenges they face. It can take various forms, from humanitarian emergency assistance to

Chapter 5

longer-term development aid. It is important that the aid goes towards targeting the specific problems of that nation. Aid comes from four main sources:

- governments of developed nations
- international organisations, for example the United Nations
- voluntary organisations, for example Oxfam
- fund-raising, for example Comic Relief.

Bilateral and multilateral aid

Aid is either bilateral or multilateral:

- **Bilateral aid** is given directly from one country to another country, for example from the UK to Tanzania.
- **Multilateral aid** is given by a group of countries to an international organisation, which then distributes the money to needy countries, for example aid given by the United Nations (UN) to Angola.

Tied aid

Tied aid is bilateral aid that, when donated, has conditions attached. These conditions stipulate that the receiving country has to use the aid to buy goods and services from the donor country. In this set-up the donor county is benefiting as well. For example, France may give €50 million to Kenya to build a hospital on the condition that a French company must build it. This is beneficial to Kenya as it is gaining a hospital, but it is also controversial as Kenya would benefit even more if it were allowed to employ its own people to do the job, which, in turn, would help its economy.

UK aid

The **Department for International Development (DFID)** is the part of the UK Government that is responsible for Britain's aid to developing countries. The focus of the department is to promote development in the developing world, particularly in countries where people are suffering from extreme poverty. The department is led by a cabinet minister, who in 2013 was Justine Greening. The DFID works with charities, business and international organisations such as the World Bank and the United Nations in working towards achieving the **Millennium Development Goals (MDGs)** (see page 98).

5 Specialist workers and experts: Teachers, trainers, medical professionals and specialist advisers can be sent. Researchers and managers are also useful as they can organise and plan training programmes.

1 Food aid: Surplus food such as cereals, powdered milk, grain and dairy products can be sent. Often, food aid is part of emergency relief aid projects.

4 Emergency relief aid: This aid is sent to assist with disasters such as earthquakes, floods and droughts. By sending immediate assistance such as tents, medical supplies, food and clothing, short-term help is given to deal with immediate problems.

Types of aid

2 Financial aid: This can involve loans of money which have to be paid back with interest; grants which do not have to be paid back; trade deals.

3 Equipment: Specialist equipment to aid development can be sent, such as vehicles, farming equipment, engineering parts, manufacturing equipment.

Figure 5.14 Types of aid

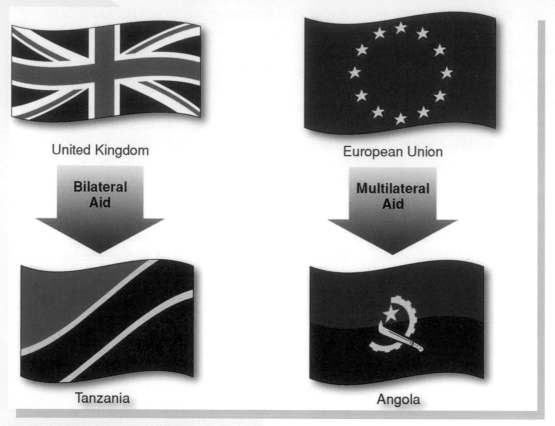

Figure 5.15 Examples of bilateral and multilateral aid

FACT FILE

The DFID

- In 2011–12, the DFID spent £7.7 billion on aid to poorer countries. Africa received £2.2 billion and Ethiopia received the largest amount, £324m.

- In 2011–12, the DFID provided bilateral assistance to 68 countries, of which 31 received direct financial aid.

- The DFID's bilateral humanitarian assistance in 2011–12 totalled £354m. The largest recipient was Somalia at £79m.

- The European Commission's development programme received the largest amount of DFID multilateral assistance (£1.2bn), followed by the World Bank (£1bn) and the United Nations (£377m).

- Much of the finance donated by the DFID comes with **political conditions**. The receiving country must be committed to tackling poverty, upholding human rights and managing public money wisely.

- By 2015 the DFID wants to secure schooling for 11 million children, save the lives of 50,000 women in pregnancy and childbirth and stop 250,000 newborn babies dying needlessly.

Case study: DFID assistance in Ethiopia

One of the biggest killers in Africa is malaria. Ten years ago, only two-thirds of Ethiopians had access to health services. Rural areas in particular suffered from a lack of medical facilities and health workers. Over the last five years, the Health Extension Program, the flagship programme of the Ethiopian ministry of health, has aimed to extend health care with a primary focus on reducing malaria cases.

DFID funding is currently supporting more than 3,900 health extension workers to deliver health services to around 9 million people in Ethiopia. Additionally, the DFID is supporting the Health Extension Program through a financial contribution to the government of Ethiopia, which pays for the delivery of services.

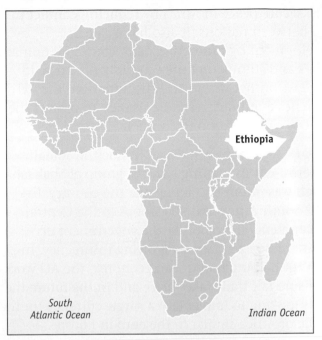

Figure 5.16 The location of Ethiopia

To what extent is aid helping developing countries?

Developed, rich nations around the world have a moral responsibility to help and assist poorer countries. Rich countries cannot sit back and watch human suffering in Africa during a famine or a flood and not step in to help. Much of the aid given by most developed countries is 'good aid'. This means it is targeted at people most in need and not tied. It also involves local people who are consulted on the most appropriate use of the money.

However, a lot of aid is still tied. Research has revealed that 80 cents out of every US dollar given in aid is returned to the USA in some way. Some countries may also deal with African nations that have dictatorships in power in order to further their own needs. For example, China provides finance and weapons to Sudan in return for oil. The government of Sudan has used these weapons to attack the non-Arab population of Darfur. For aid to work, the developing country must have a fair, open and transparent government.

Show your understanding

1 Why is providing assistance and support to African countries often difficult and complicated?
2 Read the information on types of aid in Figure 5.14 and describe them.
3 Explain the differences between bilateral and multilateral aid.
4 What is tied aid?
5 Describe the role of the DFID.
6 What assistance is the DFID giving to Ethiopia?
7 What is 'good aid'?
8 Why is it important that aid is not given to countries with dictatorships?

The work of the African Union

The African Union (AU) was founded in 2002 to help secure peace in Africa by reducing conflict in and between nations. It also has a role in development by promoting democracy and human rights and stimulating the economy of Africa. If there is conflict *within* an African nation, the AU launches a military response usually to protect the citizens of the nation in conflict.

In 2013 AU troops worked alongside the Somali Government in fighting terrorist group al-Shabaab, which was intent on taking over the country. In 2012 South Africa sent 400 troops to the Central African Republic to bolster the government of President Bozize against a growing insurgency. In terms of helping the African economy, the AU works to ensure fair trade takes place and in the future the AU is looking to implement a single currency for the whole of Africa similar to the euro in Europe.

The work of the United Nations

The United Nations (UN) plays a significant role in attempting to deal with development issues in Africa. When the UN was established in 1945, one of its main aims was to encourage countries to work together and cooperate to improve the lives of people all around the world. Nowhere is this required more than in many countries in Africa.

The UN operates a series of specialised **agencies** that work to deliver multilateral aid and assistance. Each agency has a particular focus and remit when it comes to meeting the needs of developing nations.

The United Nations Children's Fund (UNICEF) works around the world on improving the lives of children. Considering a child dies from hunger every 15 seconds in Africa, the job UNICEF does is vital in saving lives in the developing world.

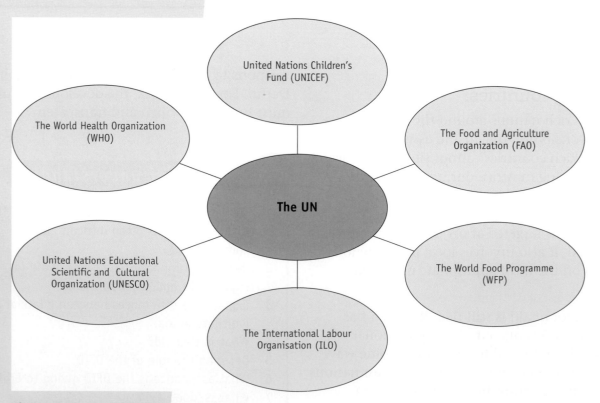

Figure 5.17 The organisation of the UN

United Nations Children's Fund (UNICEF)

UNICEF's function is to help children in need, and also to help the mothers of these children. Projects in Africa include:

- Organising emergency relief for children after a disaster.
- Working with WHO to set up medical facilities and programmes such as immunisation, birth control advice or establishing health centres.
- Helping mother and child such as its breastfeeding campaign, education campaigns and safe-motherhood campaigns.
- Working in schools to lower the high rates of illiteracy in many African countries.

The Food and Agriculture Organization (FAO)

The FAO specialises in trying to raise levels of nutrition by helping farmers improve food supplies. Projects in Africa include:

- Helping to train farmers to work on programmes to improve crop yields, nutrition levels and quality of crop.
- Researching and developing farming methods. Such projects have included irrigation schemes, using high yield crops, applying appropriate fertilisers and developing fisheries, forestry and cattle farming.
- Supplying experts, advisers and educators.

The World Food Programme (WFP)

WFP aims to save people at risk from food crises. Projects in Africa include:

- Supporting the most vulnerable groups, such as women and children.
- Helping the hungry poor to become more self-reliant by improving irrigation, food production, roads and transport.

The World Health Organization (WHO)

The WHO works to meet medical needs by promoting good health and good medical facilities. WHO projects in Africa include:

- Helping to set up health services.
- Training health professionals such as doctors, nurses, midwives and health visitors.
- Developing primary health care at local village level where hospitals and doctors are not readily available.
- Researching and working on health problems, e.g. HIV/AIDS.
- Immunisation campaigns.

The International Labour Organization (ILO)

The ILO is concerned with trying to improve working conditions. Projects in Africa include:

- Improving conditions of work including health and safety.
- Helping young children who may be forced to work long hours.
- Offering ideas, help and guidance to those who run factories and businesses.

United Nations Educational Scientific and Cultural Organization (UNESCO)

UNESCO is concerned with developing education in its broadest possible sense. Projects in Africa include:

- Encouraging governments to establish education systems which are compulsory for all.
- Sending advisers and teachers/lecturers to help create high quality schooling.
- Carrying out research in areas such as education, science and communications.
- Encouraging cooperation in arts and culture between African countries and the rest of the world.

Figure 5.18 The UN's specialised agencies

Case study: UNICEF's Schools for Africa

Figure 5.19 School children in Rwanda

UNICEF is running an international fundraising campaign called Schools for Africa to help some of the millions of children in Africa who do not get the chance to go to school because of war, poverty or discrimination. The organisation is working with governments, local authorities and communities in 11 African countries including Burkina Faso, Mozambique, Mali and Rwanda.

Since the launch of Schools for Africa, more than 12 million children are benefiting from increased access to and quality of education, improved physical and learning environments in schools and better teaching and learning processes. This has included the building of 415 new classrooms in the remotest parts of Mali and Burkina Faso, as well as the training of 10,000 teachers in Ethiopia, Mali, Malawi, Burkina Faso and Niger.

In 2000 nearly 190 countries signed up to a range of goals and targets called the **Millennium Development Goals (MDGs)**, which were designed to reduce world poverty and hunger and improve the lives of people in the developing world. Eight goals were drawn up and they have to be achieved by 2015.

The drafting of the MDGs was a great idea in principle, but progress towards achieving them has been slow in some countries and non-existent in others. The fact remains that there are still more people living in poverty in sub-Saharan Africa in 2013 than there were in 1990. Added to this, the gap between rich and poor is getting wider by the year.

FACT FILE

The eight Millennium Development Goals

1 Eradicate extreme poverty and hunger.
2 Achieve universal primary education.
3 Promote gender equality and empower women.
4 Reduce child mortality.
5 Improve maternal health.
6 Combat HIV/AIDS, malaria and and other diseases.
7 Ensure environmental sustainability.
8 Form a global partnership for development.

Show your understanding

1 Describe the work of the AU in helping Africa.
2 What was the aim of the UN when it was established in 1945?
3 **(a)** Choose three UN agencies and explain their role.
   (b) Which agency do you think does the most important job in helping Africa? Explain your choice.
4 Describe UNICEF's Schools for Africa campaign.

Branch out

5 List the eight MDGs in order of how important you feel each goal is.

Develop your skills

6 'The MDGs have been a success in helping Africa develop.' (*Mark Hughes*)

Find two reasons to oppose Mark Hughes's views.

How NGOs are helping Africa

NGOs raise funds from voluntary and private sources to fund their work in developing countries. They are not tied to any particular government or nation and they can decide for themselves what their aims and policies are. You will have seen adverts on television for various NGOs asking for donations or sponsorships. Sometimes these appear more frequently around the time of a humanitarian crisis in a developing country, such as a famine or flood.

There are many NGOs working on helping the developing world. Some focus on a particular cause such as **War Child**, whereas others operate on a broader scale such as **Oxfam**. By focusing on the work of two major NGOs, you will learn about the role they play in African development.

War Child

Figure 5.20 War Child logo

Case Study: War Child in Uganda

Uganda is a tale of two countries. The south is relatively prosperous and most children are able to attend primary school. The north, however, is a different story. In the Acholi region, more than 1 million people were forced to flee their homes by the conflict between government forces and Joseph Kony's Lords' Resistance Army. Further north still, the Karamoja region has been affected by years of tribal violence, which is now being exacerbated by climate change and the widespread ownership of guns.

What is War Child doing to help?

In Acholi, War Child has identified 2,000 of the poorest and most marginalised children (orphans and those living with HIV/AIDS) from 1,200 households. War Child is supporting people in those families to earn a decent income so they can afford to send their children to school. This involves giving training and grants to the parents, siblings (and in some cases the children themselves) to set up their own income-generating enterprises. Examples include market

Figure 5.21 Students at the opening ceremony of a new school in Acholi, northern Uganda, which is supported by War Child

stalls, bee-keeping, tailoring, livestock and agriculture production.

In Karamoja, War Child has provided 1,500 children with pens, books and uniforms to enable them to get an education. In addition, War Child trains police, local courts and medical staff to improve their work for girls who have been raped. The organisation is also providing equipment so that clinics can treat and prevent sexually transmitted infections and unwanted pregnancies.

War Child provides life-changing support to the most vulnerable children whose families, communities and schools have been torn apart by war. This includes:

- providing medical care, sanctuary and counselling to girls who have been the victim of sexual violence
- creating safe havens where children can escape the dangers of life on the streets after war has forced them to leave home
- rebuilding schools destroyed by war and getting kids out of army uniforms and into school ones
- helping children get their voices heard and their rights met, and helping local people to protect their children better.

Oxfam

Oxfam has a general aim of fighting poverty all over the world. The charity focuses its work on vital issues to tackle the root causes of poverty, from life's basics – food, water, health and education – to complex questions around aid, climate change and human rights. With this extensive field of activity, the organisation is one of the world's oldest and largest NGOs. Like other NGOs, Oxfam relies on private and voluntary donations. However, it also has a nationwide chain of charity shops in the UK that help with funding. It is also a pressure group and is proud of having thousands of members in the UK.

Figure 5.22 Oxfam logo

Case study: Oxfam in South Sudan

South Sudan is the world's newest nation, but it is also one of the poorest. After almost 40 years of civil war, water, sanitation and health services are completely inadequate. Water-related diseases are rife and one in seven children dies before the age of five.

What is Oxfam doing to help?

Oxfam is providing safe, clean water by building new watering holes in ten local communities. This means that families no longer have to walk miles to fetch water, freeing up their time for education, farming and developing livelihoods. The organisation has also ensured sustainable supplies of clean water are maintained at the water points by training 16 community teams to manage and repair wells and pumps. This, in turn, will improve sanitation and cut disease.

Figure 5.23 The Oxfam drilling team, working to find solutions to improve the water supply in south Sudan

Figure 5.24 Women and girls no longer have to spend several hours a day collecting water

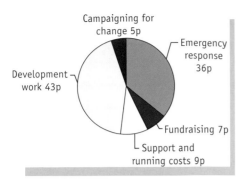

Figure 5.25 How is every £1 donated to Oxfam spent?

Africa and human rights

Human rights are universal rights that everyone is entitled to. In 1948, after the atrocities of the Second World War, the United Nations drew up a list of 30 basic rights that all humans should have.

What you will learn:

1 About the UN Declaration of Human Rights.
2 How human rights are compromised in Africa.
3 About the UN Convention on the Rights of the Child.
4 The role of pressure groups that deal with human rights.

These rights were set out in the 1948 **UN Universal Declaration of Human Rights**.

As citizens of Scotland, we can live our everyday lives without our human rights being jeopardised. However, from the selected list of human rights given in the Fact File, you will easily be able to identify numerous rights than millions of Africans will never enjoy because of the state of their nation. In every African country there will be *at least* one factor that prevents citizens accessing their full human rights as set out by the United Nations.

FACT FILE

The UN Universal Declaration of Human Rights

Here is a selected version of the Articles in the Universal Declaration of Human Rights:

1 **We are all born free and equal.** We all have our own thoughts and ideas. We should all be treated in the same way.

2 **Do not discriminate**. These rights belong to everybody, whatever our differences.

4 **No slavery.** No one has any right to make anyone a slave.

5 **No torture.** No one has any right to hurt or torture us.

7 **We are all equal before the law**. The law is the same for everyone. It must treat us all fairly.

9 **No unfair detainment**. No one has the right to put us in prison without good reason and keep us there, or to send us away from our country.

17 **The right to your own things**. Everyone has the right to own things or share them. Nobody should take our things from us without good reason.

18 **Freedom of thought**. We all have the right to believe in what we want to believe, to have a religion or to change it if we want.

20 **The right to public assembly**. We all have the right to meet our friends and to work together in peace to defend our rights.

21 **The right to democracy**. We all have the right to take part in the government of our country. Every adult should be allowed to choose their own leaders.

23 **Workers' rights**. Every adult has the right to a job, to a fair wage for their work and to join a trade union.

26 **The right to education**. Primary school should be free. We should learn about how to get on with others. Our parents can choose what we learn.

How are human rights compromised in Africa?

Children's rights

In 1989 governments worldwide promised all children the same rights by adopting the **UN Convention on the Rights of the Child**. These rights are based on what children need in order to survive, grow, participate and fulfil their potential. They apply equally to every child, regardless of who they are or where they are from. However, if a child is from Africa, the chance of them enjoying many of these rights is severely reduced.

FACT FILE

The UN Convention on the Rights of the Child

Many of the children's rights set out by the UN are the same as the Universal Declaration of Human Rights. However, there are a few additions:

- Children have the right to grow up and develop physically and spiritually in a healthy and normal way, free and with dignity.

- Children have the right to special care and protection and to good food, housing and medical services.

- Children have the right to love and understanding, preferably from parents and family, but from the government where these cannot help.

- Children have the right to go to school for free, to play and to have an equal chance to develop themselves and to learn to be responsible.

- Children have the right to be protected against cruel acts or exploitation, for example they shall not be obliged to do work that hinders their development, both physically and mentally.

- Children should not work before a minimum age and never when that would hinder their health, and their moral and physical development.

- Children should be taught peace, understanding, tolerance and friendship among all people.

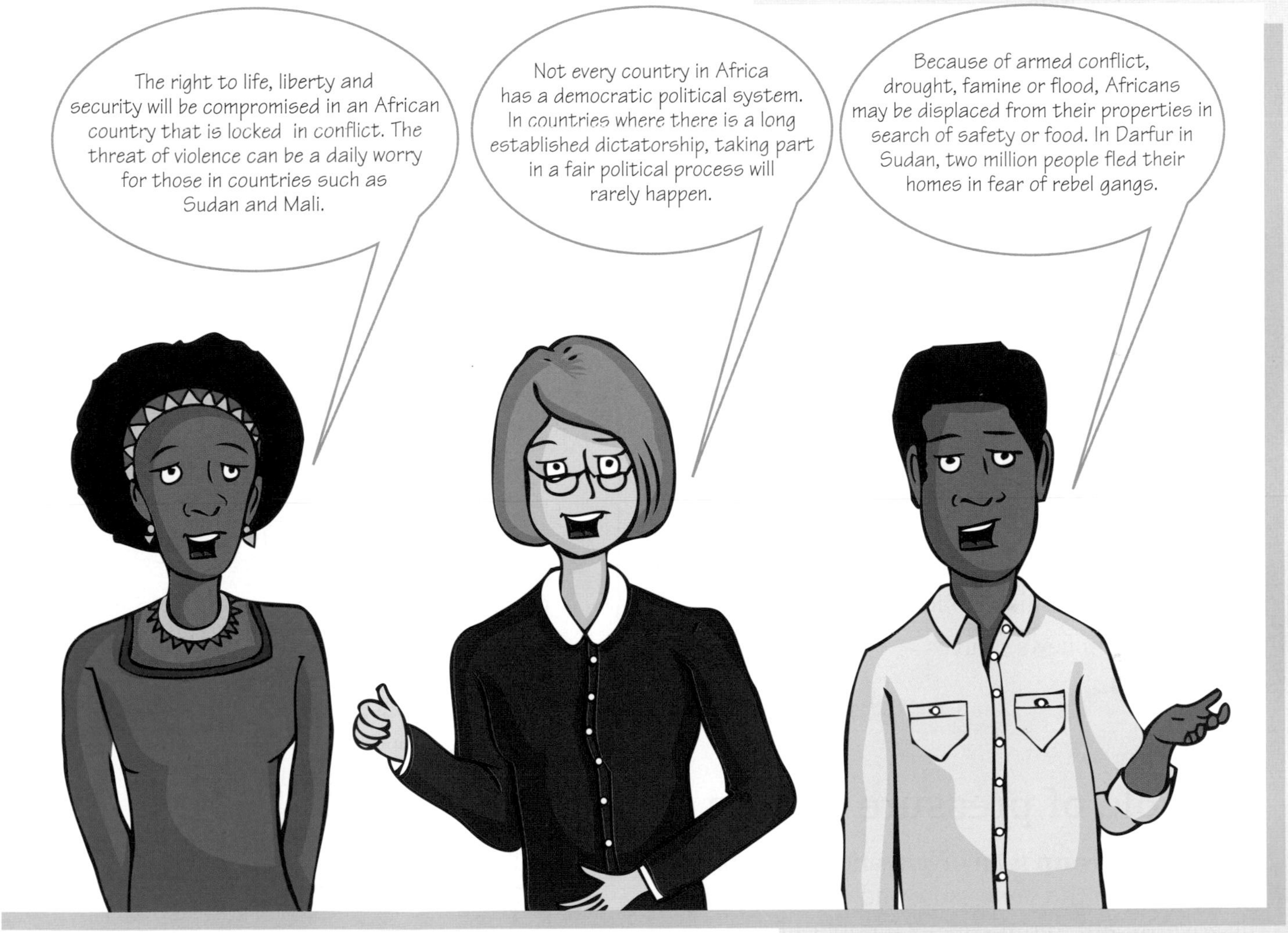

Figure 5.26 How are human rights compromised in Africa?

END CHILD LABOUR IN GOLD MINES

The uneven ground of the mining village of Kollo, near the border between Burkina Faso and Ghana, is busy with workers smashing boulders into pebbles with basic hammers and sticks. About thirty of them are children. They are also required to lift heavy buckets of water from the well up the hillside, and then sift through the mud, searching in the silt for tiny flecks of gold.

Close by is a hill, with entrances to mine shafts dug 50 metres into the ground. Matthew, aged 12, finds his way down into the mine. It is a hazardous journey, finding slippery footholds in poor light in extremely narrow spaces. After 20 minutes he reaches the bottom and fills his bucket with ore, to be hauled up by ropes.

Children here don't go to school and suffer ill health working in such dangerous conditions. Much of this work is prohibited under international law for anyone under 18 but it is estimated one million children in Africa are working in mines like Kollo.

Adapted from news sources

The role of pressure groups

A **pressure group** is an organisation of people who believe in the same cause and wish to influence the government and the general public. There are many well-known pressure groups that aim to promote human rights, highlight human rights abuses and hold governments to account over their human rights records. **Amnesty International** is a worldwide pressure group that works to protect people wherever justice, fairness, freedom and truth are denied. It works to bring about change relating to human rights around the globe.

WWW

Go to the Human Rights Watch website at www.hrw.org to carry out further research into human rights in Africa.

Show your understanding

1   What are human rights?
2   **(a)** What is the UN Declaration of Human Rights?
    (b) Choose the three human rights set out in the UN Declaration of Human Rights that you feel are the most important. Explain your choices.
3   **(a)** What is the UN Convention on the Rights of the Child?
    (b) Choose two of the rights set out in the Convention on the Rights of the Child that you feel are the most important. Explain your choices.
4   Read the information on child labour in gold mines.
    (a) Describe what Matthew is made to do in the mine.
    (b) What evidence is there to suggest the work is dangerous?
    (c) Why is working in the gold mines a risk to children's health and education?
5   What is the aim of pressure groups that deal with human rights?

Added value

Investigate human rights abuses in an African country of your choice. You could focus on a target group such as children or on a particular right that is being abused.

Chapter 6

International terrorism

What is terrorism and what are its causes?

What is terrorism?

Terrorism is a difficult concept to understand and label. When looking at it from the outside, it could simply be seen to be a group or organisation scaring, injuring or killing innocent people. However, by studying terrorism in more depth you will begin to realise that behind every terrorist act there is a motive or various motives. These motives tend to be associated with **nationalist**, **political** or **religious goals**.

Terrorism itself differs from the general idea of war. During a war, military groups (armies) try to avoid civilian casualties in pursuit of the enemy. However, terrorists deliberately target innocent people, believing that it will better advance their cause. They also do this because terrorist groups are usually small and not able to achieve their goals through fighting with a national army. In targeting and killing innocent people, they attempt to create a climate of **fear and instability** in society. Terrorists then hope their tactics will lead to public outcry and the achievement of whatever goals they demand. Terrorist attacks over the past decade have increased, with countries around the globe targeted from Scotland to Indonesia. Attacks also take many forms, including suicide bombing and kidnapping, and for this reason terrorists are often referred to as **extremists**.

What are the causes of terrorism?

It is important to note that terrorist acts are generally *not* committed for financial gain. An attack is defined as a terrorist attack if it is

> **What you will learn:**
> 1 The definition of terrorism.
> 2 What the causes of terrorism are.

committed with the aim of achieving nationalist, political or religious goals. The causes of terrorism may overlap; for example, a terrorist group may be active because of religious hatred and nationalist or political goals.

Nationalism

Nationalism is relevant in the UK and is best understood when thinking about our own country. Scotland is part of the UK and has been since 1707, but some people in Scotland believe the time has come for our country to become an independent nation separate from the UK. These people can be described as **nationalists**. Scotland may well become an independent nation with Scottish nationalists achieving their goals through politics in a peaceful manner.

> **Nationalism** is a view that that independence should be sought because of a common culture, heritage and language.

However, there are other people around the world who live in countries or regions that want independence but feel they cannot achieve it peacefully. These people, therefore, decide to turn to violence and terrorism to try to achieve their nationalist goal. These people are also sometimes referred to as **separatists**.

Politics

Around the world there are countries that do not have the same political system as the UK. In the UK we have a **democracy** where every citizen has a voice. However, there are other countries that are run by **dictatorships** or corrupt governments. These oppressive governments make decisions that are not fair on the majority of people who live there and, as there are no elections, they are in power for many years. In countries such as these, groups of citizens, known as **rebels**, may resort to terrorist activities to try to bring about social and political change within their country. As much as these groups may be engaging in terrorist activities, they may actually have widespread support among the population. The civil war in Syria is one example of such a situation.

Religion

Religion has been associated with terrorism for centuries. Close to home, the 'Troubles' in Northern Ireland always had a religious slant and since 9/11 (see page 109) the role of religion as a cause of terrorism is greater than ever before. People who commit terrorist attacks in the name of their religion are referred to as **religious extremists**. Behind the 9/11 terrorist attacks, and indeed many terrorist attacks of the last decade, were Islamic religious extremists. These extremists are angry about **the West**'s involvement in affairs in the Middle East such as the wars in Iraq, Afghanistan and the Israeli–Palestinian conflict. They believe the Western way of life is very different to life in a Muslim country and do not want Westerners in their land. Islamic extremists are therefore waging a **jihad** (holy war) against the West, believing that they are acting on behalf of Allah (God) to fulfil a duty. In carrying out terrorist attacks, Islamic extremists believe they become **martyrs** and will be rewarded in the afterlife.

> **The West** is a term used to describe European countries and the USA, and those countries around the world that support 'the West' such as Australia.

Other contributing factors

Terrorists may also be driven by a sense of relative **deprivation** and **poverty** within their society. **Globalisation** and modern media have given people in less developed nations an acute awareness of their situation compared to those enjoying high living standards in the developed world. Seeing the economic and social differences between themselves and the Western world can infuriate some in underdeveloped countries, increasing tension and hostility.

> **Globalisation** is the process by which the world is becoming increasingly interconnected through trade, travel, culture and communication.

One example of this situation is currently happening in Somalia, where most of the current generation of Somalis have grown up in conditions of conflict, insecurity of livelihood and deprivation. This has tended to make many of them vulnerable to the arguments and promises of militant group **al-Shabaab**.

Discrimination can also lead to terrorism. If a person from a particular racial, religious or ethnic group within a country faces discrimination, this can lead to a feeling of isolation and alienation. The person may then seek out communities with cultures like their own. These groups may become jaded towards society and, in turn, become **radicalised** in retaliation to the discrimination they have faced.

> **Radicalisation** is a process where a person or group increasingly adopts extreme political, social or religious views or ideas.

Show your understanding

1 What is the difference between war and terrorism?
2 Why do terrorists target innocent people?
3 What is an extremist?
4 'Terrorists do not have any goals; they just attack innocent people at random.' Do you agree with this statement? Justify your answer.
5 Describe why nationalism and poverty might lead to terrorism.
6 Why are Muslim extremists waging a war against the West?

Branch out

7 Create a detailed mind map displaying the causes of terrorism.

Case study: The Israeli–Palestinian conflict

Figure 6.1 The conflict between Israel and Palestine has existed for over 60 years

The conflict between Israel and Palestine has raged for over 60 years. The causes of the conflict are complex, but ultimately they include nationalist, political and religious reasons.

Background

At the heart of the conflict is what both sides believe. The Israelis believe they are entitled to an area of land now known as Israel, while Palestinians believe they are entitled to the same area of land they call Palestine. Unfortunately, both sides claim the same land; they simply call the land by different names. To add to this situation, there is a religious aspect too.

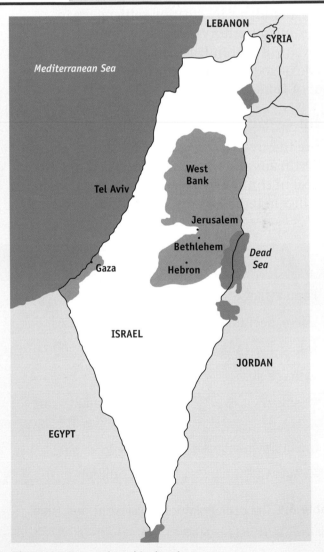

Figure 6.2 Israel and Palestine

Jewish Israelis believe the land was given to them by their God, and Muslim Palestinians believe it was given to them by their God. Both peoples believe the land is their **holy land**.

When Israel was created in 1948, Palestine lost large areas of land. At this stage there was an attempt to create two nations but the Palestinians were dissatisfied with their share. Palestine now consists of two relatively small areas of land known as **Gaza** and the **West Bank**. Ever since 1948, both countries and their populations have been fighting over territory and Israel has been accused of taking more land from the Palestinians by creating settlements in Palestinian territory. Israel also controls movement within Palestinian territories and the trade of goods (food, medicine, weapons) in and out of Palestine.

The conflict

Since the creation of Israel in 1948, the Palestinians and the Israelis have been in almost constant conflict with each other. It is an unfair conflict in terms of power. Israel is a rich country with a powerful military and Palestine is very poor with no military. Conflicts in recent times have reflected this, with Palestinian rebels resulting to terrorist tactics against the Israeli state.

Over the last few years there has been an escalation of fighting in the Gaza area, a small area of land densely populated by 1.7 million Palestinians. Palestinian rebel fighters have fired rockets into Israeli towns and attacked Israeli soldiers. In retaliation, Israel has conducted airstrikes and fired shells into Gaza. Israel has come under severe criticism for its excessive military response as it has often killed more Palestinian civilians than rebel fighters. In 2012 Israel airstrikes killed over 100 civilians including children.

This type of conflict is ongoing, with no sign of compromise ahead. The USA is working to try to end the conflict and Barack Obama has asked for the building of Israeli settlements in Palestine to stop. However, the USA continues to support Israel, providing it with over $3 billion in military aid in 2012.

	Palestine	Israel
Population	4 million	7.7 million
Life expectancy	74 years	81 years
Infant mortality rate	17 deaths/1,000 births	4 deaths/1,000 births
Average age	18 years	29 years
Literacy	92% of adults can read and write	97% of adults can read and write
Unemployment rate	26%	5.6%
Annual GDP	£4.2 billion	£153 billion

Table 6.1 The demographics of Palestine and Israel

Source: *CIA World Factbook*

Show your understanding

1. Read the case study on the Israeli–Palestinian conflict.
   (a) Why are the two countries engaged in conflict? Answer fully.
   (b) Why is the conflict 'unfair'?
   (c) Why has Israel come under severe criticism?
   (d) Discuss the following quote with your teacher: 'One man's terrorist is another man's freedom fighter.'
2. Using Table 6.1, describe the differences between Palestine and Israel.

Terrorism and its impact on the world

What you will learn:

1. The events of major terrorist attacks.
2. Who al-Qaeda are.
3. About terrorist activity in North Africa.
4. How terrorism has changed the world.

Terrorism has become a major issue in society since the terrorist attacks on the USA on 11 September 2001. Since 9/11 various terror attacks have occurred throughout the world giving birth to the idea of **international terrorism**. Terrorism is now a worldwide issue and not just confined to countries locked in conflict. For the citizens of Scotland, terrorism became a very real experience when Glasgow Airport was attacked in 2007 by two men linked to the terrorist group al-Qaeda.

Major terrorist attacks

9/11

Figure 6.3 The 9/11 attacks on the USA by the terrorist group al-Qaeda

The most infamous of terror attacks were those on the USA by the Islamic terrorist group al-Qaeda, led by Osama bin Laden.

On the morning of 11 September 2001, 19 terrorists affiliated with al-Qaeda hijacked four passenger jets. The terrorists crashed two planes into two skyscrapers at the **World Trade Center** in New York City. The impact and fire eventually caused the buildings to collapse with 2,752 people still inside. A third plane was crashed into and destroyed part of the **Pentagon** (the US military headquarters) in Washington, killing 190. The fourth plane crashed in the countryside just outside Pittsburgh, Pennsylvania, following a struggle between the hijackers and passengers. Officials believe that the terrorists on that plane intended to crash into the White House. In all, nearly 3,000 people were killed in the 9/11 attacks, with al-Qaeda deliberately targeting key symbols of US power.

Case study: Al-Qaeda

Al-Qaeda was founded in the late 1980s by **Osama bin Laden**. The group practises an extreme version of Islam. It is intensely opposed to the USA and other Western democratic nations. Members are especially against the presence of these Western countries in Arab nations near the Islamic holy land. As well as being based in Afghanistan, al-Qaeda has **underground cells** in dozens of countries around the globe from Britain to Somalia. In these countries, especially in the Middle East and Africa, militants are trained and radicalised to become extremists. Because of the nature of the organisation, al-Qaeda is very difficult to fight in a traditional war and therefore very difficult to defeat or stop.

In 2011 al-Qaeda's founder and leader, Osama bin Laden, was found in Pakistan and assassinated by US Special Forces (see page 117).

As well as 9/11, al-Qaeda has been linked to other terrorist attacks:

★ 1992: its first terrorist attack took place as two bombs were detonated in Yemen

★ 1993: World Trade Center bombing

★ 1998: US Embassy bombing in Kenya and Tanzania

★ 2002: Bali bombings

★ 2004: Madrid bombings

★ 2005: London bombings

★ 2007: Glasgow Airport attack

★ 2008: Danish Embassy bombing in Pakistan

★ 2013: Algerian gas plant hostage crisis; Boston Marathon attack; terrorist murder of soldier in London; Kenya shopping mall attack.

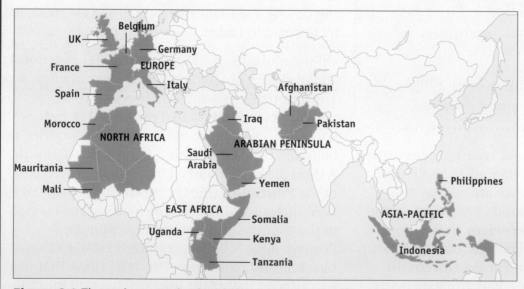

Figure 6.4 The main countries in which al-Qaeda operates

Show your understanding

1 Explain why terrorism is now considered a worldwide issue.
2 (a) Which terrorist group was behind 9/11?
  (b) Describe, in detail, the events of 9/11.
3 Read the case study about al-Qaeda.
  (a) Who founded the terrorist group and when?
  (b) Describe the members' beliefs.
  (c) Is al-Qaeda an international organisation? Explain your answer.

Branch out

4 Write a newspaper article describing the events of the day on 9/11.

Figure 6.5 The 7/7 bombings in London

The London bombings of 7/7

On 7 July 2005, one day after it was announced that London would host the 2012 Olympics, four suicide bombers detonated three bombs on the London underground and one on a London bus. The co-ordinated attack happened during the morning rush hour when millions of commuters were making their way to work and school. The three bombs on the underground exploded on trains just outside Liverpool Street and Edgware Road stations, and on another travelling between King's Cross and Russell Square. The suicide bombers detonated the bombs all within 30 seconds of each other, showing this attack was well planned.

The fourth and final explosion was around an hour later on a double-decker bus in Tavistock Square, not far from King's Cross. In total, 52 people were killed and over 770 injured. The four terrorists were all young men aged between 18 and 30 years old. Police believe they were motivated by a hatred of the West and the UK's foreign policy towards the Middle East. It is also believed that the men may have been radicalised through the Internet by visiting extremist websites and learning how to make bombs.

Glasgow Airport terror attack

On 30 June 2007, two terrorists crashed a Jeep Cherokee packed with gas canisters into the main terminal of Glasgow Airport. As the Jeep rammed into the terminal, hundreds of families were queuing to check in.

Fortunately, the Jeep became wedged in the terminal doors restricting entry to the building. When this happened the two terrorists got out and tried to set both the jeep and the gas canisters alight. The jeep, as well as the terminal building, caught fire but the gas canisters did not explode. The two men, who were dressed in boiler suits, were also on fire as it became apparent to onlookers that this was indeed a terrorist attack and not an accident. The police and civilians managed to detain the terrorists and prevent them from harming any innocent people inside the airport.

Both men, Bilal Abdulla and Kafeel Ahmed, were doctors and highly educated. They carried out the attack as they believed the West was to blame for invading Iraq and the deaths of thousands of Muslims. Kafeel Ahmed only lived for four weeks after the attack and eventually died in hospital of 90% burns. Bilal Abdulla survived and was sentenced to 32 years in prison for conspiracy to commit mass murder.

Figure 6.6 The attack on Glasgow Airport, June 2007

Figure 6.7 Drummer Lee Rigby

Boston and London, 2013

The events of Boston and London in 2013, less than two months apart, highlight how vulnerable the West is to terrorist attacks.

In April, at the finishing line of the Boston Marathon, two bombs exploded killing three people and injuring over 100. The perpetrators of this horrific act were the Tsarnaev brothers who were originally from the Chechnen republic of Russia. The two Muslims had become radicalised and had links with al-Qaeda. In a shoot-out with the police, one of the brothers was killed and the other was eventually found and taken to hospital in a serious condition.

The random murder in a busy London street in May 2013 of Lee Rigby, aged 25, shocked the nation and represented a new phase in terrorist attacks. The young soldier attacked was wearing a T-shirt in support of Help for Heroes, a military charity. The attack took place a few hundred metres from the Royal Artillery Barracks. He was first run over by the terrorists' car and then brutally hacked to death. The two assailants, both covered in blood, remained in the street chanting 'Allahu Akbar' – 'God is great'. Both were eventually shot and wounded and charged with murder. The terrorists, both in their early 20s, had been brought up as Nigerian Christians but had been converted to Islam and **jihadist** extreme views.

Terrorist activity in North Africa

Over the last decade the threat of terrorism has traditionally come from Afghanistan and Pakistan. However, over the last few years there has been a shift towards increased terrorist activity in North and East Africa. Al-Qaeda groups have grown in countries like Somalia and Mali (see Figure 6.4), where they are able to take advantage of the lack of infrastructure and policing. They are able to recruit and train in the desert and move freely without restrictions from the law or the army. The **Algerian hostage crisis** in January 2013, where 38 people were killed including six Britons, led Prime Minister David Cameron to declare that North Africa is now a major focus for counter-terrorism efforts.

In September 2013, another terror attack struck Africa, this time in Nairobi, Kenya. Al-Shabaab terrorists took siege of an upmarket shopping mall executing unarmed men, women and children as they tried to hide or flee. The siege went on for over 4 days as the Kenyan police and military fought against the terrorists. The aftermath left 68 people dead including six Britons.

ICT task

Research a major terrorist attack such as 9/11, the London bombings or the Boston Marathon attack. Create a PowerPoint presentation to explain what happened, who was responsible and what the terrorists' motives were.

Added value

Research a terrorist group and study its motives for committing terrorist attacks. Outline the impact that the group has had on the country in which it originates or on the world. Possible groups to study include al-Qaeda, ETA or al-Shabaab.

How has terrorism changed the world?

The world has changed dramatically since the events of 9/11. Britain is at war in the Middle East along with the USA, supporting the **War on Terror**. Terrorism remains a threat in Western nations and consequently Western governments have increased security measures to reduce this threat. For example, during the 2012 Olympic Games in London, the government brought in 3,500 extra troops to guard Olympic venues and authorised a military aircraft carrier on the River Thames. Furthermore, we all now have to live with the risk of terrorism in our day-to-day lives and this can cause fear and anxiety among the population. Within Western societies there has been an increase in **Islamophobia** since 9/11.

The way in which we travel has also changed, with increased security at UK airports. Before 9/11, passengers were allowed on planes with hand luggage containing objects such as scissors or large bottles of water. Now there are restrictions on hand luggage to avoid the threat of a terrorist boarding a plane with explosives. Passengers also have to pass through strict security systems. Heathrow Airport in London operates a **biometrics system** that scans passengers' eyes and can identify them against a database. You will also notice a visible armed police presence in most airports, with police always prepared and ready for terrorist-related incidents.

Figure 6.8 Security on high alert during the 2012 London Olympics

Show your understanding

1 What is Islamophobia?
2 Describe two ways in which the world has changed since 9/11.

Islamophobia is a prejudice against, hatred towards or irrational fear of Muslims.

ICT task

Go to www.911educationprogramme.co.uk to further investigate 9/11.

Responses to the threat of international terrorism

What you will learn:

1 How the UK has responded to terrorism.

2 How the international community has responded to terrorism.

The UK's response to terrorism

The world has changed as countries around the globe have responded to the threats of terrorism. Some of these responses will be obvious to you and others less so. The fact remains that terrorism can impact our lives at any point and so governments must make sure that they are not only prepared and responsive to potential attacks but are also working actively to prevent the growth of terrorism in the first place.

The War on Terror

The **War on Terror** was launched in 2001 in the aftermath of 9/11 and in response to the increasing threat of terrorism. It was started by the USA with the support of Britain and other countries. The War on Terror involved an international military campaign to eliminate al-Qaeda and other terrorist organisations, beginning with the **invasion of Afghanistan** in search of Osama bin Laden. The War on Terror

continues today albeit under the command of US President Barack Obama, who does not refer to it using the same name. The USA and the UK still have a large military presence in Afghanistan and are continuing to fight an ever-expanding network of terrorist organisations. At the end of 2012, David Cameron stated that the UK would be reducing the number of troops in Afghanistan from 9,000 to 5,200 by the end of 2013 as the country moves towards stability.

Figure 6.9 UK troops fighting terrorism

The cost of the War on Terror has been substantial, with the USA spending around $4 trillion according to academic experts and the UK spending around £20 billion since 2001. The human cost to the UK has also been distressing, with over 600 soldiers killed in Iraq and Afghanistan since 2001.

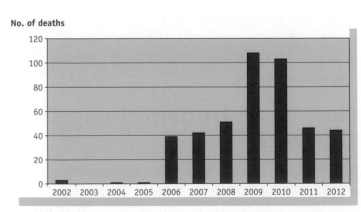

Figure 6.10 UK military deaths in Afghanistan, 2002–12

Counter-terrorism

Many governments around the world now have counter-terrorism strategies in place. These work to stop terrorism *before* attacks take place. The UK Government's counter-terrorism strategy is called **CONTEST** and it has four main aims:

- The government **pursues** terrorists and disrupt their work.
- The government **prevents** terrorism by countering the various factors that cause people to become terrorists.
- The government **protects** the public through increased vigilance and security.
- The government prepares for and **minimises** the potential harm caused by terrorist attacks if they do occur.

The Scottish Government works within this strategy and operates its own special counter-terrorism unit called the Scottish Preventing Violent Extremism Unit (SPVEU).

MI5

MI5, the **British Security Service**, has seen its role, staffing and budget increase significantly because of the increasing threat of international terrorism. At MI5's headquarters a special department called the Joint Terrorism Analysis Centre (JTAC) was established in 2003. This department works to gather and assess all information related to terrorism at home and overseas. It is also responsible for setting the UK terrorist **threat level**. There are five levels of threat:

- critical – an attack is expected imminently
- severe – an attack is highly likely
- substantial – an attack is a strong possibility
- moderate – an attack is possible but not likely
- low – an attack is unlikely

WWW

Visit the UK Home Office website at www.gov.uk/terrorism-national-emergency to see what the current threat level is.

Deportation of suspected terrorists

As part of counter-terrorism strategy, the UK Government may work to deport people whom they suspect of being linked to terrorism. In October 2012 **Abu Hamza**, an Egyptian-born Muslim fundamentalist, was deported from the UK to the USA where he was wanted for crimes linked with al-Qaeda such as setting up terrorist-training camps. Another Islamic fundamentalist, **Abu Qatada**, was arrested in London in October 2002 and here he began a long legal battle against deportation. It was more than ten years before he was finally sent back to Jordan, after the UK and Jordanian governments agreed that evidence gained through torture would not be used against him in his forthcoming trial.

The role of the police

The role of the police in society has changed with the threat of terrorism. Police forces have officers who are trained specifically in counter-terrorism and forces such as the Metropolitan Police have an **anti-terrorist hotline** where members of the public can phone to report terrorist-related incidents or suspicions. Furthermore, the police track online terrorist activity, known as **cyber-terrorism**. The Internet is used by some people to promote, glorify or help carry out acts of terrorism and violent extremism. The use of the Internet allows terrorists to reach a wide audience and the police monitor social media as well as extremist websites.

> ### ➡ Added value
>
> 'The War on Terror has been unsuccessful in fighting the growth of terrorism.' Research and investigate the arguments for and against this statement. You could present your findings in a word-processed booklet illustrated with tables, graphs and images.

Show your understanding

1 (a) Why did the USA (with the support of the UK) launch the War on Terror and what was its aim?

(b) What has the financial cost of the war on terror been to the USA and the UK?

2 (a) What is counter-terrorism?

(b) Describe the UK Government's CONTEST strategy.

3 (a) Describe how MI5 has adapted in response to the threat of terrorism.

(b) What does it mean if the UK has the following terrorist threat levels?

(a) moderate

(b) substantial

(c) critical

4 How has the role of the police changed to combat terrorism?

5 What is cyber-terrorism?

Develop your skills

6 Using Figure 6.10, reach a conclusion about the number of UK military deaths in Afghanistan between 2002 and 2012.

The international response to terrorism

The USA

Since 9/11 the USA has been the country that has led the fight against international terrorism. Initially launching the War on Terror in an attempt to capture those responsible for 9/11, the USA now operates against any terrorist activity that may threaten world peace. In this role the USA has become the **'world's policeman'** in combating terrorism, but this role is controversial and many argue that the USA is increasing terrorist activity as opposed to stopping it. The very presence of the US Army in the Middle East is enough for some extremists to wage war against it.

Guantanamo Bay

Guantanamo Bay is a US-run **detention camp** or prison based in Cuba. It was opened in 2002 by the

Case study: US drone attacks

The USA has increasingly used unmanned aerial vehicles, known commonly as **drones**, to target terrorists living in remote areas in countries such as Pakistan and Afghanistan. Drones have multiple uses, from gathering intelligence to surveillance, listening to mobile phone conversations and actively attacking suspected terrorists. In December 2012 a US drone missile killed three al-Qaeda militants in Yemen including a senior member, Saleh Mohammed al-Ameri.

However, the use of drones has been controversial as they spread fear among the general public of countries in the Middle East. The reason for this fear is understandable: drones have killed hundreds of innocent people in the hunt for suspected terrorists. It is this sort of tactic employed by the USA that is said to fuel terrorism.

Figure 6.11 A US drone plane

George W. Bush Government to hold detainees suspected of terrorist-related activity or crimes. The prison is highly controversial as it detains suspects without trial and has been accused of torturing detainees. Currently there are 166 people held at Guantanamo. Some of them have been there as long as 11 years, without ever having been charged. In 2013 around 100 prisoners went on hunger strike in protest at their detention and treatment.

Case study: The death of Osama bin Laden

Figure 6.12 Osama bin Laden

After searching for a decade, in 2011 US Special Forces found and killed al-Qaeda's leader and 9/11 mastermind, Osama bin Laden. He was located and found living in a quiet area of Pakistan called Abbottabad. After several months of surveillance and planning, a team of US Navy Seals carried out a daring midnight raid on bin Laden's compound. At 12.30 a.m. on 2 May 2011, 25 commandos landed in two Black Hawk helicopters and entered bin Laden's house. They shot him twice, killing him instantly. His body was then taken to Afghanistan for identification before being buried at sea. This was to prevent his grave becoming a shrine for extremists.

In the fight against terrorism, the killing of bin Laden was a major breakthrough for the USA and the international community. He was not only the head of al-Qaeda; he was also seen by extremists around the world as the leader in the fight against the West.

When Barack Obama came to power in 2008, he vowed to shut Guantanamo Bay but in 2013 it remains open. In April 2013, in reaction to the hunger-striking situation, Obama said Guantanamo 'must close' as it was 'a recruitment tool for extremists and contrary to who we are as a nation'. It remains to be seen if Obama will be successful in his goal. See pages 121–122 regarding the debate surrounding suspected terrorists and human rights.

Show your understanding

1. Why is the USA referred to as the 'world's policeman' and why is this role controversial?
2. Read the case study on the death of Osama bin Laden.
   - **(a)** In detail, describe his assassination.
   - **(b)** Why did the USA dispose of his body at sea?
   - **(c)** Why was the death of bin Laden seen as a breakthrough in the War on Terror?
3. **(a)** What is the purpose of Guantanamo Bay?
   - **(b)** Why is Guantanamo Bay controversial?

Develop your skills

4. 'US drone attacks have been very successful in the war against terrorists.' (*Paul Daly*)
   Using the case study on US drone attacks, give one reason to support and one reason to oppose the view of Paul Daly.

Increased international cooperation

As well as countries individually fighting terrorism, there are a number of international organisations that try to help prevent and stop terrorist attacks on their members. The United Nations, the North Atlantic Treaty Organization and the European Union are three important international organisations that fight terrorism.

The United Nations (UN)

Almost every country in the world is a member of the UN. In joining the UN, countries sign up to the collective aim of working together to maintain peace and security throughout the world. Through the UN the international community has agreed on a **global strategy** to combat terrorism.

Figure 6.13 The UN logo

The aims of the UN global strategy against terrorism include:

- to promote a culture of peace and respect among nations, religions and people
- to ensure that no country is facilitating, financing or providing a base for terrorist activity
- to intensify cooperation in exchanging timely and accurate information concerning the prevention and combating of terrorism
- to strengthen co-ordination and cooperation among member nations in combating crimes that might be connected with terrorism, such as drug trafficking and arms trading

North Atlantic Treaty Organization (NATO)

Figure 6.14 The NATO headquarters in Brussels

Like the UN, NATO was created after the Second World War with the aim of avoiding any future wars. It is made up of 28 countries that have a **military** and **political alliance** with each other. The idea is that countries that are part of NATO will defend each other against attack and work together to increase security and peace.

Since 9/11 NATO has a new role in fighting terrorism around the world. Alongside the US-led military campaign in Afghanistan, NATO has been leading the **International Security Assistance Force (ISAF)** that is tasked with assisting the government of Afghanistan in creating a stable nation. The ISAF represents NATO's determination to help the people of Afghanistan build a stable, secure and democratic state free from the threat of terrorism. This includes creating a political system with free and fair elections, as well as training the Afghan police and military to ensure the rule of law in society.

The European Union (EU)

The European Union works to reduce the threat of terrorism in EU countries. Cooperation between states is key, as is the sharing of terrorist-related intelligence. When a terrorist attack happens in an EU country, other member nations work to assist with the response. An EU database lists the resources and assets that nations could mobilise in the case of a terrorist attack. Furthermore, **Europol** (the European law-enforcement agency) works to make Europe safer by assisting the member nations of the EU in the fight against serious international crime and terrorism. Europol uses the expertise of 700 staff to identify and track the most dangerous terrorist networks in Europe. Law enforcement authorities in the EU rely on this intelligence work and the services of Europol to carry out almost 12,000 cross-border investigations each year. These have led to the disruption and arrest of thousands of potential criminals and terrorists.

ICT task

Go to the website of either the UN, NATO or the EU and create an information leaflet on how the organisation of your choice works to combat terrorism.

1   Describe how the following international organisations work to combat terrorism:
(a) The United Nations
(b) NATO
(c) The European Union.

How does terrorism impact the human rights of civilians around the world?

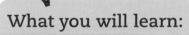

What you will learn:

1   About the UN Declaration of Human Rights.

2   How terrorism affects human rights.

3   About human rights in Afghanistan.

4   The debate surrounding human rights and terrorists.

5   The role of pressure groups that deal with human rights.

Human rights are universal rights that everyone is entitled to. In 1948, after the atrocities of the Second World War, the United Nations drew up a list of 30 basic rights that all humans should have. These rights were set out in the 1948 Universal Declaration of Human Rights. See page 103 for a simplified list of these rights.

How does terrorism affect human rights?

The very nature of terrorism aims to destroy human rights, upset society, destabilise governments and spread fear among populations. Terrorism has a direct impact on the enjoyment of a number of human rights, in particular the rights to life, liberty and security. No matter who you are or where you are from, as a human being you should be entitled to live your life peacefully without the threat or fear of associated terrorist crimes such as bombings, murder, intimidation or kidnapping. As citizens of Scotland we can live our everyday lives without our human rights being jeopardised by terrorist-related crime, although it is always a possible threat. However, living peacefully without fear is only a distant dream for many people around the world who live in countries continually affected by terrorist activity.

Case study: Human rights in Afghanistan

Before 2001, Afghanistan was under the rule of the **Taliban**, which ran the country using an extreme form of Islamic shariah law. The people of Afghanistan, especially women, had very few human rights under this system. Restrictions included banning people listening to music, watching television or using the Internet. Women had to be covered from head to toe, were not allowed to work, to play sports or to wear make-up.

Since the US-led invasion, progress has been made on human rights as the country is now under the control of a democratic government. However, compared to Scotland, human rights in Afghanistan are still extremely poor. Despite the progress made, significant challenges remain and divisions exist in Afghan society over issues such as women's rights, religious freedom and freedom of expression. The Taliban, which is now considered a terrorist organisation, still operates in many parts of the country and it tries to reverse the progress made on human rights.

Case study: Malala Yousafzai

Malala Yousafzai (born 1997) is a Pakistani school pupil and education activist. She is known for her education and women's rights activism in the Swat Valley, where the Taliban had at times banned girls from attending school. In 2009, at the age of 11–12, Malala wrote a blog under a pseudonym for the BBC detailing her life under Taliban rule, their attempts to take control of the valley, and her views on promoting education for girls. At the time, Taliban militants were taking over the Swat Valley, banning television, music, girls' education and women from going shopping.

Figure 6.15 Malala Yousafzai

On 9 October 2012, a masked Taliban gunman shot Malala in the head and neck as she rode home on a school bus. Six days later, she was flown to the UK for treatment. The assassination attempt sparked a national and international outpouring of support for Yousafzai. UN Special Envoy for Global Education Gordon Brown launched a UN petition in Malala's name, using the slogan 'I am Malala' and demanding that all children worldwide be in school by the end of 2015.

On 12 July 2013, Malala's 16th birthday, she spoke at the UN to call for worldwide access to education.

The UN dubbed the event 'Malala Day'. It was her first public speech since the attack:

'The terrorists thought they would change my aims and stop my ambitions, but nothing changed in my life except this: weakness, fear and hopelessness died. Strength, power and courage was born ... I am not against anyone, neither am I here to speak in terms of personal revenge against the Taliban or any other terrorist group. I'm here to speak up for the right of education for every child. I want education for the sons and daughters of the Taliban and all terrorists and extremists.'

Show your understanding

1 What are human rights?
2 **(a)** Refer to page 103 and choose three of the selected human rights from the UN's Declaration that you feel are the most important. Explain your choices.
   (b) From the rights you have chosen, write down the responsibilities that would accompany these rights.
3 How does terrorism impact on people's human rights?
4 Read the case study on human rights in Afghanistan.
   (a) What progress has been made with human rights in Afghanistan?
   (b) What rights are still debated there?
5 Read the case study on Malala Yousafzai. Why was she shot and by whom?

Branch out
6 Write a few paragraphs outlining the main differences in human rights between Scotland and Afghanistan.

Do terrorists and criminals have human rights?

Every person is entitled to the same basic human rights as set out by the United Nations. These rights also apply to suspected terrorists. Many people would argue that a person suspected or convicted of mass murder should not be entitled to any human rights at all.

Everyone has differing views on the application of human rights when it comes to terrorists. The UK has been accused of being a 'soft touch' in terms of dealing with suspected terrorists, as we observe human rights laws stringently. Consider the arguments given in Table 6.2.

The role of pressure groups

A pressure group is an organisation of people who believe in the same cause and wish to influence the government and the general public. There are many well-known pressure groups that aim to promote human rights, highlight human rights abuses and hold governments to account over their human rights records. These pressure groups play an important role and aim to reduce the threat of terrorism through the spreading of **peaceful resolution**. Pressure groups such as **Liberty** and **Amnesty International** work to prevent anyone, including convicted criminals and terrorists, from suffering human rights abuses such as unfair imprisonment, torture or execution.

THREAT TO THE UK BUT NO TO DEPORTATION

A court has ruled that Al-Qaeda operatives Abid Naseer and Ahmad Faraz Khan could not be deported because it would infringe their human rights. The pair were planning a 'mass casualty attack' against shoppers at the Arndale Centre in Manchester over the Easter holiday last year.

Judges said that Naseer, 24, and Faraz Khan, 26, who came to Britain as students, should not be sent back to Pakistan because of the risk that they could be tortured. Britain, under EU human rights law, has been heavily criticised for protecting terrorists and disregarding the safety of the British public all in the name of human rights.

Adapted from news sources

For human rights	Against human rights
Everyone should be innocent until proven guilty. We cannot presume people are terrorists.	If the police strongly suspect someone is a terrorist, we should put them in jail just in case they carry out an attack.
In the UK we have abolished the death penalty and should look to life imprisonment instead.	People who have killed dozens of people in terrorist attacks should not have the right to life. They should receive the death penalty for taking the lives of others.
No one should be subject to torture – it is inhumane and derogatory.	We should subject terrorists to torture to find out more information about their networks and organisations.

Table 6.2 Examples of views for and against human rights for suspected terrorists

Show your understanding

1   Consider the views expressed in Table 6.2. Outline your own views on whether terrorists should have their human rights respected or not.

2   Read 'Threat to the UK but no to deportation' on page 121. Should these two men have been deported? Justify your answer.

3   What is the aim of pressure groups that deal with human rights?

Branch out

4   Working in pairs, create a table outlining the arguments for and against human rights for terrorists.

ICT task

Go to Liberty's website at www.liberty-human-rights.org.uk or Amnesty International's website at www.amnesty.org.uk and research how they protect people's human rights. Create a four- to six-slide PowerPoint presentation to give to your class.

Chapter 7

Assessment: National 4 & 5 Skills and Knowledge

Welcome to National 4 and National 5 Skills and Knowledge!

You should now have the skills and knowledge to complete the assessment demands of the International Issues unit of the Modern Studies course. The skills and knowledge required for National 4 and National 5 are very similar, with National 5 requiring you to handle more detailed sources and to display greater detail in your knowledge answers.

National 4 Assessment

The National 4 award for Modern Studies is assessed by your teacher and not graded by an external marker. To achieve the award you need to pass the internal assessment for each of the following units:

N4

- Democracy in Scotland and the United Kingdom
- Social Issues in the United Kingdom
- International Issues
- National 4 Added Value assignment.

National 5 Assessment

The National 5 award is made up of both internally and externally marked assessments. To achieve the award you need to pass the internal assessment for each of the following units:

- Democracy in Scotland and the United Kingdom
- Social Issues in the United Kingdom

N5

- International Issues.

The Added Value for National 5 Modern Studies is an externally assessed course assessment. This consists of two parts:

- National 5 question paper
- National 5 assignment.

In Modern Studies we look at a range of issues that affect everyone's lives. These issues are based on evidence gathered through research carried out by a whole series of people and organisations – from governments to charities. As part of your qualification you will be expected to carry out a piece of personal research on a particular topic which is relevant to what you have studied. This is called the **Added Value unit assignment** at National 4 and the **assignment** at National 5.

How do I carry out a piece of research?

When researching a topic in Modern Studies, it is important to consider where you will get your information from. In the twenty-first century you have access to huge amounts of information at your fingertips on the Internet. However, you need to be conscious of its accuracy and its likelihood of containing bias.

Where do I gather information from?

The information gathered from research can be broken down into two parts: primary information and secondary information.

Primary information

Primary information is evidence that you have gathered by yourself and is unique to your personal research. Your personal research should be based around at least two pieces of information gathered by primary research as well as information gathered from other sources. The ways in which you gather evidence can vary greatly – some examples are below.

- Surveys / questionnaires
- Interviews
- Emails
- Letters
- Focus groups
- Field studies

Secondary information

Secondary information is evidence that you have gathered from research that was carried out by others. You should use it to help support your personal research. There are vast amounts of secondary information available, in many different formats – below are just a few examples.

- Newspapers, magazines and books
- Internet search engines and websites
- Television and radio programmes
- Mobile phone apps
- Social media such as Twitter
- Library books and articles

How do I plan my research?

In order to carry out a successful piece of personal research you need to plan it effectively. You will need to keep all evidence of your planning so that your work can be assessed.

Topic/Issue

You should agree an issue to research with your teacher. It must relate to one or more of the issues that you have studied in your course, so it is a good idea to pick something from one of the three units you have studied:

- Democracy in Scotland and the United Kingdom
- Social Issues in the United Kingdom
- International Issues.

Hypothesis

If you are being presented at National 5 and you have decided on your topic/issue, then you may state a hypothesis which you will revisit in your conclusion. A hypothesis is simply a statement that your personal research will help prove or disprove.

Sources of information

You may wish to consider the following questions about your primary and secondary sources.

- What useful information have I got from this source to help me research my issue?
- How did I collect this information or where did it come from?
- How reliable is the information gathered from the source?
- Could the source contain bias or exaggeration?

Background knowledge

What relevant knowledge do you have from your Modern Studies course which will help you research your issue?

Conclusions

Using all of the information gathered, what are your final thoughts on your issue?

Presentation

How are you going to present your sources and findings? You could choose the following methods of presenting your Added Value assignment:

- **Oral presentation** – you may want to give a 5-minute talk to the class. This talk should be well organised and can be supported with other materials such as a PowerPoint or Prezi. You could include a question and answer session at the end of your presentation.

- **Written report** – you may wish to submit a structured essay/report or mock newspaper article. You could also create an online blog or wiki to present your findings.
- **Display** – you could create a large and well-structured poster incorporating your findings. After presenting it to the class you could hold a question and answer session.
- **Audio recording** – you could create a scripted podcast to present your findings. The podcast could include interviews or could take the form of a radio broadcast.
- **Video recording** – you may want to create a video recording to help present your findings. You could create a mock news broadcast or a short film and even use software such as iMovie and Movie Maker to create a presentation.

Sample plan

Below is an example of how a piece of personal research could be planned and structured. You should work with your teacher to consider how you should structure, plan and carry out your own piece of research.

Poster presentation

Area of course: International Issues

Topic/Issue: The effects of gun use in the UK and the USA

Hypothesis: *The abuse of gun ownership is a major problem in the USA but not in the UK.*

Introduction: In this section I will explain why I chose the topic and how I collected my information.

Display: In my poster I will include 4 sources of information – the results of a survey/questionnaire, the transcript of an interview with a focus group, a section on secondary sources I used and, lastly, a section on my own knowledge.

Source 1 – Survey/Questionnaire

I am going to ask my friends, neighbours and family to respond to the following questionnaire. From the questionnaire I will create a bar graph of responses to the key question. I will then give some of the reasons for people's responses and discuss whether the findings of the questionnaire agree or disagree with my hypothesis. Using the questionnaire, I could also gather evidence to show whether people believe that the abuse of gun ownership is a major problem in the USA but not in the UK.

This is what my survey may look like:

Gender	Male			Female	
Age	12–17	18–24	25–40	41–60	60+
Do you think the use of guns is a major problem in the USA but not in the UK?			Yes	No	Undecided
Give one reason for your answer					

This is what my graph may look like:

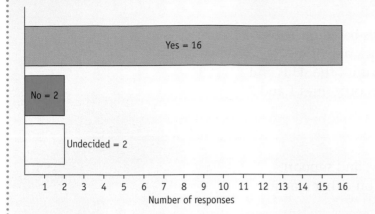

Yes = 16

No = 2

Undecided = 2

1 2 3 4 5 6 7 8 9 10 11 12 13 14 15 16
Number of responses

Source 2 – Interview with a focus group

Using my mobile phone, I will record a discussion session with a focus group of 3 of my classmates. I will ask the following question:

Why is gun ownership such a problem in the USA but not in the UK?

I will then type up a transcript of the discussion to display on my poster and I will highlight any arguments which agree or disagree with my hypothesis.

My transcript may look like this:

Me: Do you think that the ownership of guns makes citizens safer in the USA than in UK?

Person 1: I think that guns are too easily available in the USA – look at the December 2012 killings of those primary schoolchildren by a deranged gunman.

Person 2: Yes, but many Americans claim it's their constitutional right to own a gun.

Person 3: We need to compare the number of individuals per 10,000 population killed by guns in the UK and the USA.

Source 3 – Secondary sources

In this section of my poster I will include a newspaper article on the topic that I have found and also selected evidence from the BBC website which provides information on the number of deaths by guns.

Source 4 – My own knowledge

The final source section of my poster will be based on my own knowledge of the topic. I will organise this into arguments which agree or disagree with my hypothesis.

Research methods: For each source I will consider the relevance, the accuracy and whether they could contain bias.

Conclusion: At the bottom of my poster I will have my conclusion, which will consider whether my hypothesis of *The abuse of gun ownership is a major problem in the USA but not in the UK* has been proved or disproved.

National 4 International Issues
Assessment items

At National 4 you will be expected to answer a skills-based question/ activity and knowledge and understanding questions/activities. For the internal assessment of this international issues unit, the skills and knowledge which will be assessed are as outlined in outcomes 1 and 2 below.

Outcome 1

- Ability to use two sources of information to draw and support conclusions about international issues focusing on either a major world power or a significant world issue.

Outcome 2

- Straightforward description and brief explanations demonstrating knowledge and understanding of international issues, focusing on either a major world power or a significant world issue.

Assessment evidence

Evidence for successful completion of both outcomes can be based on a range of activities:

- responses to questions
- a presentation
- information posters, or
- participation in group tasks.

The examples that follow are based on written responses.

National 4 World Powers: USA

Skills Question

Study Sources 1 and 2 below, then answer the question that follows.

Source 1

A viewpoint on gun crime

Fifty-five million kids went to school on the day that 20 were massacred at Sandy Hook Elementary in Newtown, Connecticut. Even in the USA, therefore, the chances of a child dying in a school shooting are remote. Is gun violence increasing in the USA? The overall rate of violent crime has fallen by 22% in the past decade (and 18% in the past five years).

Seventy mass shootings have occurred in the USA since 1982, leaving 543 dead. These crimes were horrific, but 564,452 other murders took place in the USA during the same period. Mass shootings scarcely represent 0.1% of all murders.

Source 2

Murders in the USA, 2010

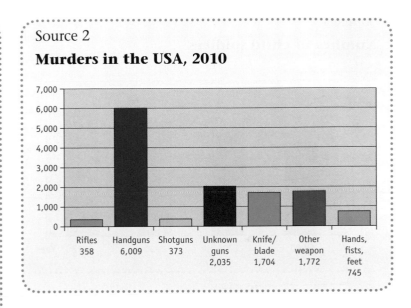

Using sources 1 and 2, what **conclusions** can be drawn about murders in the USA?

You should reach a conclusion about the following:

- the number of mass shootings compared to overall murders
- weapons used in murders.

Your answer must be based only on the information in the sources.　　　　　　　　　　**(4 marks)**

Knowledge and Understanding Question

In the USA, people can take part in politics in various ways.

(a) Describe **two** ways in which people can take part in politics in the USA.　　**(4 marks)**

There are many reasons why some ethnic minorities experience inequalities in education.

(b) Give **two** reasons why ethnic minorities may experience inequalities in education.　　**(4 marks)**

National 4 International Issues: Global Issues

Skills Question

Study sources 1 and 2 below, then answer the question that follows.

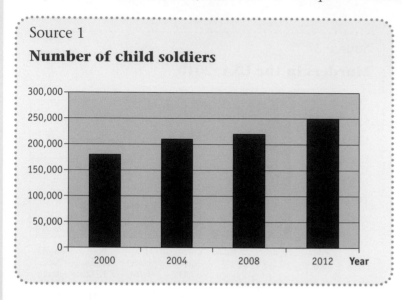

Source 1

Number of child soldiers

Source 2

Child soldiers

Children who live in countries that are underdeveloped and locked in armed conflict may find themselves caught up in war as child soldiers. These children are forced to kill and do things no child should be forced to do. Child soldiers are found in many countries all over the world, but most are in Africa in countries such as Somalia and Uganda.

Using sources 1 and 2, what **conclusions** can be drawn about child soldiers in Africa?

You should reach a conclusion about the following:

- the numbers of child soldiers
- where child soldiers are found

Your answer must be based only on the information in the sources.   **(4 marks)**

Knowledge and Understanding Question

Terrorism has changed the world in the last decade.

(a) Describe **two** ways the world has changed due to the threat of terrorism.   **(4 marks)**

Africa has the largest number of child soldiers of any continent.

(b) Give **two** reasons why there are so many child soldiers in Africa.   **(4 marks)**

National 4 Added Value Unit

The assignment

The Added Value Unit will be internally marked by your teacher. The SQA's unit specification document states that in order to pass the assignment you must research and use information relating to a Modern Studies topic or issue by:

- **Choosing, with support, an appropriate Modern Studies topic or issue.** You should choose an issue that you are interested from any part of the course. Below are some examples from the International Issues unit:
  - Gun ownership is a problem in USA but not in the UK.
  - South Africa is a stable and successful democracy.
  - The American Dream is not a reality for many US citizens.
  - The War against Terror has been won.
  - Civil war is the major reason why some African countries are poor.
- **Collecting relevant evidence** from at least two different sources. The section on research methods (see page 124) provides useful information on the types of sources that can be used.

- **Organising and using information** collected to address the topic or issue. You should use your skills to decide if the information is balanced or biased and based on fact rather than opinion.

- **Using the knowledge and understanding** you now have to describe and explain the key learning points you wish to make.

- **Applying your Modern Studies skills** in detecting bias or exaggeration, making decisions and drawing conclusions.

- **Presenting your findings and conclusion** on the issue you have chosen. You can present your findings in a variety of ways: as a written piece of research, or a poster, or a talk followed by questions, or you can use digital media such as a blog or journal.

National 4 Added Value Checklist

Name			
Title			
Unit(s)	Democracy in Scotland and the United Kingdom	Social Issues in the United Kingdom	International Issues
Relevant sources of information			
Number and type			
Evidence evaluated			
Skills used			
Detecting bias and exaggeration			
Making decisions			
Drawing conclusions			
Type of presentation			
Written report			
PowerPoint			
Wall display/Other			
Conclusion/Findings			
Based on evidence			
Evidence of individual work (if task is a group/ paired activity)			

N4

National 5 International Issues

Assessment items

At National 5 you will be expected to answer a skills-based question/ activity and knowledge and understanding questions/activities. For the internal assessment of this international issues unit, the skills and knowledge which will be assessed are as outlined in outcomes 1 and 2 below.

Outcome 1

- Ability to use a range of sources of information to draw and support conclusions about international issues, focusing on either a major world power or a significant world issue.

Outcome 2

- Detailed description and explanations demonstrating knowledge and understanding of international issues in the United Kingdom, focusing on either a major world power or a significant world issue.

Assessment evidence

Evidence for successful completion of both outcomes can be based on a range of activities:

- responses to questions
- a presentation
- information posters, or
- participation in group tasks.

The examples that follow are based on written responses.

National 5 World Powers: South Africa

Skills Question

Study Sources 1–3 below, then answer the question that follows.

Source 1

Education issues in South Africa

Since the end of the apartheid, progress has been made in improving education. Schools can no longer base their selection of pupils on race. Many black, coloured and Asian children now attend the former white state schools or private schools. In 2011 the government invested 21% of the entire budget on education. Compulsory education begins at age 7 (Grade 1) and ends at age 15 (Grade 9).

Free schooling has been introduced for the poorest 40% of students (all educated in black-only schools). The target is to increase this figure to 60%. It is hoped this will encourage more black students to stay on at school. The Afrikaans Teachers' General Secretary stated that in 1997 1.6 million pupils started primary school, yet in 2009 only 370,000 completed their matriculation exam.

Exam results have improved: in 1995 fewer than 50% of students passed and by 2011 it was 70%.

The number of students sitting the new National Senior Certificate (matriculation exams) has increased in recent years. In 2004 the number of students sitting the exams was 400,000; by 2009 it had risen to 570,000. However, inequalities remain between the poorer rural provinces like Eastern Cape and Mpumalanga and the urban richer provinces such as Western Cape and Gauteng. Again, racial differences in education still remain: most white children achieve high exam results and are educated in schools with excellent resources, whereas most black children achieve poor exam results and are educated in schools with limited resources.

Improvements in the condition of schools have taken place over the years. In 2002, 38% of schools had no electricity but by 2010 this figure had dropped to 18%. President Zuma has set a target to eliminate all mud huts in rural South Africa by 2012.

Source 2

School attendance and matriculation pass rates

Province	Children aged 7–15 attending school (%)	Pass rate in the matriculation exam (%)
Gauteng	99.0	75.0
Western Cape	98.5	82.0
Eastern Cape	97.4	56.7
Free State	96.5	71.0
North West	96.0	69.0
KwaZulu-Natal	96.0	68.0
Northern Cape	95.5	70.0
Limpopo	92.5	64.5
Mpumalanga	92.0	55.0

Source 3

Percentage pass rates for matriculation and higher entry education by race, based on schools in Mpumalanga province

Race	%
Matriculation:	
Asian/Indian	90
Black	60
White	100
Coloured	80
Higher education:	
Asian/Indian	19
Black	10
White	40
Coloured	8

Using sources 1–3, what **conclusions** can be drawn about education in South Africa?

You should reach a conclusion about each of the following:

- racial differences in education
- provincial differences in education
- improvements in education over time.

Your conclusions must be supported by evidence from the sources. You should link information within and between sources in **support** of your conclusions. Your answer must be based on all three sources. **(8 marks)**

Knowledge and Understanding Question

Housing conditions in urban areas have improved.

(a) Describe, **in detail**, two ways in which housing conditions have improved. **(6 marks)**

Poor health is still suffered by many people in South Africa.

(b) Explain, **in detail**, why many South Africans suffer poor health. **(6 marks)**

National 5 International Issues

Skills Question

Study sources 1–3, then answer the question that follows.

Source 1

Terrorist activity around the world in 2012

The international community has had some success in recent years in the battle against terrorism. This has resulted in the number of terrorist related incidents worldwide dropping from a high in 2008 to 10,178 in 2012. The number of incidents in individual countries has also come down, with the number in Afghanistan decreasing. However, the number of terrorist incidents in Somalia and Spain has increased, which is a worrying trend. In Somalia much has to be done to return the rule of law to society as the country is suffering from political and economic failure.

The motives for terrorist incidents varied from country to country. In both Afghanistan and Pakistan, the most common motive for terrorism was religious. This is due to Islamic extremism in these countries. In Spain, nationalism was the main motive. The number of deaths caused by terrorism remains high although the number of terrorist incidents has dropped. More people died in a terrorist incident in Afghanistan than anywhere else, whereas the USA was the safest place from terrorism. In Pakistan, a high number of deaths were caused by suicide attacks and car bombings.

(N5)

Source 2

(a) The number of terrorist incidents worldwide, 2008—12

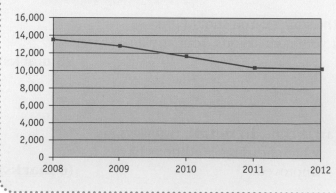

(b) Terrorist incidents in selected countries, 2010 and 2012

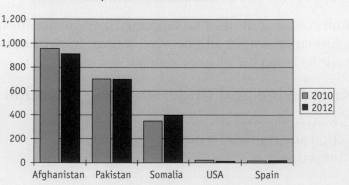

Source 3

(a) Motive for terrorist incidents, 2012

	Religion	Nationalism	Political	Other
Afghanistan	546	179	156	31
Pakistan	478	102	98	23
Somalia	125	80	91	2
USA	4	1	5	2
Spain	4	11	2	1

(b) Deaths caused by terrorist incidents, 2012

Country	Number of deaths
Afghanistan	2193
Pakistan	1898
Somalia	1012
USA	8
Spain	11

Using sources 1–3, what **conclusions** can be drawn about terrorism around the world?

You should reach a conclusion about each of the following:

- changes in the level of terrorist incidents worldwide
- motives behind terrorist incidents in selected countries
- the levels of terrorist incidents in selected countries.

Your conclusions must be supported by evidence from the sources. You should link information within and between sources in **support** of your conclusions.
Your answer must be based on all three sources. **(8 marks)**

Knowledge and Understanding Question

There are various factors that cause terrorism.

(a) Describe, **in detail**, the causes of terrorism. **(6 marks)**

Many countries in Africa suffer from civil war.

(b) Explain, **in detail**, why some counties in Africa suffer from civil war. **(6 marks)**

National 5 Course Assessment

Added Value is assessed in the course assessment and is made up of two components:

- a question paper with activities from each of the three units
- National 5 assignment.

Course Assessment Structure

Component 1: Question paper

The question paper is worth a total of 60 marks, with 20 marks for each unit of the course. Overall, 26 marks are for skills and 34 marks are for knowledge and understanding.

Component 2: Assignment

The assignment is worth a total of 20 marks. Of these, 14 marks are for skills and 6 marks are for knowledge and understanding.

Total marks available   80 marks

To gain the course award all units and course assessments must be passed. The mark you achieve in the question paper and assignment are added together and an overall mark will indicate pass or fail. From this, your course award will then be graded.

National 5 Assignment

The National 5 assignment is a personal research activity which must include at least two methods of collecting information with comment on the effectiveness of the methods used. The information collected should display knowledge and understanding of the topic or issue chosen. The results of the search will be written up under controlled examination conditions. As previously mentioned, 20 marks are given to the assignment.

Preparation for the assignment

1 Research topic/issue

You should choose an appropriate topic or issue, for example, *NATO should be abolished* (see page 131 for examples of other topics). You may choose an issue from any of the three individual units or you may choose a topic that integrates two units of the course, for example, *The abuse of gun ownership is a major problem in the USA but not in the UK*. The best practice is to present the research question in the form of a hypothesis with a clear aim.

2 Research methods

As part of your assignment, you must gather relevant evidence to support your hypothesis using at least two methods of collecting information. There is a range of methods you could use, including field work, referencing books or the Internet. You are expected to evaluate the strengths and weaknesses of each research method you use and to analyse your findings. Remember that two methods are the minimum you are required to use and you might wish to widen your range to more than two.

3 Research findings

This is the section which will display your detailed knowledge and understanding in describing and explaining issues relevant to your hypothesis, including identification of a variety of viewpoints. Here you must also evaluate the evidence you have gathered and describe what it shows.

4 Research conclusions

Once you have successfully analysed and explained the information you have gathered, you should make conclusions based on your research. Your conclusions must be relevant to your research issue and link back to your original hypothesis. Try to avoid simply repeating the findings you have previously given.